150 Easy Classic Chicken Recipes

Delicious Chicken Recipes For All Occasions - Quick and Easy

Bonnie Scott

ISBN-13: 978-1494235017

TABLE
OF
CONTENTS

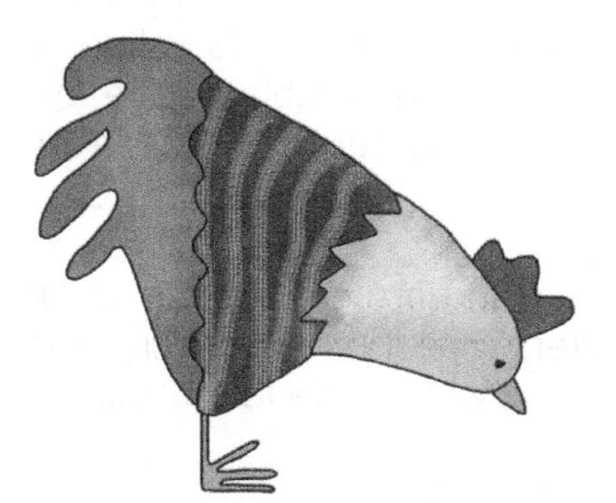

Show Me the Chicken!

Chicken Cooking Tips

- Boneless chicken cooks far more quickly than bone-in chicken, so when you're pressed for time, opt for boneless cutlets or pieces.

- Lay chicken between sheets of plastic wrap when you're flattening it with a mallet. It helps to keep the meat from disintegrating, and you can easily make it a uniform thickness.

- The easiest way to cut chicken into fingers or bite size pieces is when the chicken is barely frozen. If you're using fresh meat, put it in the freezer just until it's just hardened. If you are using frozen meat, partially defrost it. You will be able to slice it quickly and evenly with no squishing or oozing.

- If you're having problems cutting up fresh chicken, try cutting it with household scissors. Kitchen shears are a simple and effortless way to cut up those slinky, slippery pieces of raw meat.

- If your recipe calls for cooked chicken, poach the chicken instead of boiling it. Boiling can toughen the meat, while gently poaching it until done will keep it moist and tender. Use herbs, vegetables, juice, broth or white wine in your poaching liquid to add flavor to your meat.

- If you're planning on rubbing or coating your chicken pieces with oil or butter, wipe the pieces dry with a paper towel so the coating will adhere to the skin.

Chicken Grilling Tips

- If you're grilling boneless chicken that varies in thickness from one side to the other, use a mallet to flatten it, so the entire piece of meat will cook evenly.

- Leave the skin on the meat while grilling. You can slide a knife between the meat and skin to create a pouch that can hold herbs and seasonings. You can even use it to hold a bit of butter for added juiciness.

- Wait until the last five minutes of cooking to use a basting sauce that has sugar, honey or molasses in it. The sugar content of the sauce burns easily, and you'll end up with blackened chicken whether you intended to or not.

- Use tongs to turn your meat on the grill. Piercing the flesh with a fork allows the juices to escape, and you'll end up with a dry, unappetizing entrée.

Tips for Sautéing Chicken

- When you're sautéing, you move your food while it is cooking while allowing it to brown on all sides. A small amount of fat or other oil is used to cook your meat at a relatively high heat in a shallow pan. This differs from frying, in which ingredients are fully cooked and browned on one side before turning to cook the other side. More oil may be used to facilitate this so the ingredients don't stick to the pan.

- Don't use a non-stick pan when sautéing. The point of the exercise is for the meat to brown and develop more flavor, and non-stick surfaces don't brown as well or as easily.

- Don't be a sissy about the temperature at which you're cooking. A moderately high heat will brown and cook the meat quickly, and since you're standing right there tossing it, your ingredients won't stick. Quick cooking also keeps the meat tender, so you're not chewing jerky when you sit down to eat.

- Dry your chicken with a paper towel before placing it in the hot pan so it doesn't spit and steam.

- If you are sautéing a chicken breast, place the meat between layers of plastic wrap and pound to a uniform thickness. The meat will cook all the way through and you won't end up with chewy, over-done thin edges.

- Crowding your ingredients causes the chicken to steam, and your meat won't brown. If necessary, cook your chicken in several batches to prevent steaming.

Tips for Stir-Frying Chicken

- Sautéing and stir-frying are similar, but there are definite differences. The first difference is that the temperature for stir-frying is extremely hot. The second difference is that your food will be cooked, but it will not be browned. This ultra-quick cooking prevents moisture loss from your ingredients.

- After you have added oil to your wok, swirled it around to coat the surface of the pan. After it is hot, add flavorings such as garlic, chilies and ginger and stir until you can smell the aroma of the seasonings. At that point, begin adding your vegetables and meat. The essence of the seasonings will permeate your other ingredients more fully when they have had time to release their flavors.

- Constant motion keeps your meat from sticking, so don't even think about walking away from the stove while you're stir-frying. You won't have time anyway, as the chicken will cook in just three to five minutes.

Tips for Braising and Stewing Chicken

- Braising and stewing are very similar. The biggest difference is that stewing usually involves bite-size pieces and a lot more liquid. It's not mandatory to brown your ingredients before stewing, but it adds to the flavor of your finished dish.

- Use a heavy pan or skillet with a tight-fitting lid to braise your meat. You'll want to use the same pan that you browned the ingredients in to complete the cooking, as you'll get maximum flavor from the browned bits and scrapings left in the braising pan when you make your sauce.

- Make sure the oil is hot before placing your chicken in the pan so it doesn't absorb excess oil.

- Don't overcrowd the pan with too many pieces of chicken, as this causes steaming and prevents proper browning.

- Do not boil your food. Keep the temperature at a low simmer. This keeps the meat from turning dry and stringy.

- You can finish cooking your meal on top of the stove or in the oven. The oven method envelopes the entire pan with even heat, so this technique prevents the bottom from burning. You won't need to monitor your cooking for scorching.

Tips for Roasting and Baking Chicken

- Roasting and baking are both done in the oven using the dry heat method. Roasting generally means cooking in an open pan, and often the meat is set above the pan on a rack so it doesn't simmer in its own juices. Roasting also usually uses a higher temperature to brown the outside of the meat. This seals the surface to hold in the juices. Often roasting is a two-prong proposition. The initial oven temperature is set very high to brown the meat, and then the temperature is lowered to finish the cooking process. Baking usually uses a lower cooking temperature and the addition of cooking liquid for casseroles and other dishes.

- Store-bought rotisserie chicken tastes so good because it's been well seasoned before roasting. Brine your chicken to add flavor, moisture and tenderness. Add approximately 3/4-cup kosher salt to a gallon of cold water. Then add your favorite herbs, fruit juice and even some sugar to help the skin brown. Submerge your chicken and put in the refrigerator for anywhere from 2 to 12 hours. When you're ready to cook your meal, dry the chicken thoroughly and dispose of the brine solution.

- Stuff your whole chicken with fresh herbs, fruit slices and savory vegetables like onion, celery and garlic before roasting to add flavor to every bite. Remove and discard the stuffing before serving your meal.

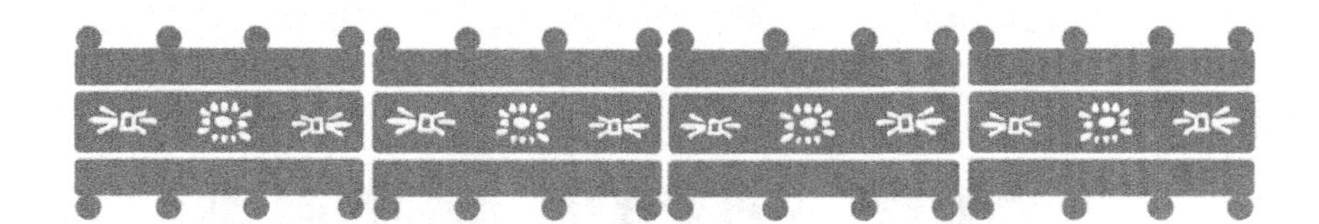

Boneless Chicken from the Oven

Chicken from the Oven – Boneless

Sour Cream Chicken

4 boneless, skinless chicken breast halves
1/8 teaspoon salt
1/8 teaspoon pepper
1/8 teaspoon garlic powder
1/4 cup melted butter or margarine
1 (10.5 oz.) can cream of mushroom soup
1 (8 oz.) carton of sour cream
1/2 cup cooking sherry
1 (4 oz.) can button mushrooms
1/8 teaspoon rosemary
1/8 teaspoon tarragon

Grease shallow casserole dish. Season chicken with salt, pepper and garlic powder. Arrange chicken in dish; drizzle melted butter or margarine over chicken. Mix soup, sour cream, sherry, mushrooms, rosemary and tarragon. Spread over chicken. Bake uncovered 1 1/2 hours at 350 degrees F. Yield: 4 servings.

Stuffed Chicken Breasts

8 boneless, chicken breast halves with skin left on
1 medium onion, finely chopped
1 tablespoon butter
1 (10 oz.) package frozen, chopped spinach, thawed and drained
1 lb. whole-milk ricotta cheese
1 egg, slightly beaten
1/4 cup parsley, chopped
1 tablespoon oregano
Salt and pepper to taste
1/8 teaspoon nutmeg

Sauté onions in butter until soft. Remove from heat and combine with spinach, ricotta cheese, egg, parsley, oregano, salt and pepper and nutmeg to make filling.

Place each chicken breast skin side up on a board. Loosen skin from 1 side of breast and stuff 1/3 cup of filling under the skin. Tuck the skin and meat under the breast forming an even, round, dome shape. Put stuffed breasts in a buttered baking dish. Fifteen minutes before baking preheat oven to 350 degrees F. Bake until golden brown, 30 to 35 minutes. Cool slightly before serving. Yield: 6 to 8 servings.

Chicken Tetrazzini

1 (8 oz.) package of linguine or spaghetti, briefly boiled, do not fully cook
4 boneless, skinless chicken breast halves
2 tablespoons olive oil
1/8 teaspoon salt
1/8 teaspoon pepper

Cream Mixture:
2 tablespoons margarine or butter
1 cup flour
4 cups milk
1 cup heavy cream
1 cup chicken broth
1/8 teaspoon nutmeg

Mushroom Mixture:
1 cup button mushrooms, chopped
1/2 cup onion, chopped
Minced garlic, to taste
1/2 cup white wine
Fresh thyme, pulled off stems & chopped

3/4 cup frozen peas
1/4 cup fresh parsley, chopped
1/3 cup Italian-style bread crumbs
1/4 cup slivered almonds
1/2 cup freshly grated Parmesan cheese
2 tablespoons margarine or butter

Preheat oven to 425 degrees F. Sauté chicken breasts in olive oil and salt and pepper until fully cooked; shred chicken.

In a saucepan, combine margarine or butter, flour, milk, cream, broth and nutmeg. Bring to a boil, whisking occasionally. Reduce heat and simmer for 5 minutes.

Sauté mushrooms, onion, garlic, wine and thyme together. Mix shredded chicken, cream mixture and onion-mushroom mixture with the linguine. Add peas and parsley. Top with bread crumbs, almonds and Parmesan cheese. Dot with butter. Bake for 25 minutes at 425 degrees F. Yield: 4 servings.

Chicken Lasagna

3 cups cooked, diced chicken
1 (8 oz.) package lasagna noodles, cooked & drained
1 (10.5 oz.) can cream of mushroom soup
2 (10.5 oz.) cans cream of chicken soup
1/2 cup grated Parmesan cheese
1/2 cup sour cream
1/4 cup mayonnaise
1 teaspoon garlic salt
2 to 3 cups shredded Mozzarella or Cheddar cheese

Mix the soups, Parmesan cheese, sour cream, mayonnaise and garlic salt together in a bowl. Spray a 9x13-inch pan with non-stick cooking spray. Put 1/3 of the soup mixture in bottom of pan, then 1/3 of the chicken and mozzarella or cheddar cheese. Layer cooked noodles on this mixture.

Continue in the same manner with the second and third layers. Top with remaining cheese. Cover and bake at 350 degrees F for 45 minutes. Let stand for 10 minutes before cutting and serving. Yield: 4 servings.

Lemon-Cream Chicken

8 boneless, skinless chicken breast halves
Flour
Salt and pepper to taste
2 eggs, beaten
3 tablespoons margarine
Juice of 1 lemon
1 pint heavy cream
3 tablespoons Worcestershire sauce
2 tablespoons dry mustard
1/2 teaspoon paprika
Cooked brown rice

Dip chicken breasts in flour, salt, pepper, and then in beaten eggs. Place chicken in a baking dish and dot with margarine. Pour lemon juice on top of chicken. In a bowl, mix together cream, Worcestershire sauce dry mustard and paprika. Pour over chicken and bake for 1 hour at 350 degrees F. Serve with hot cooked brown rice. Yield: 4 to 6 servings.

Zesty Chicken and Rice

4 boneless, skinless chicken breast halves
2/3 cup uncooked rice
1 cup French fried onions
1/2 teaspoon Italian seasoning
1 3/4 cups chicken bouillon
1/3 cup Italian dressing
Vegetables (frozen or fresh)
1/2 cup French fried onions

In a bowl, combine rice, French fried onions, Italian seasoning and chicken bouillon; pour into a 13x9-inch baking dish. Arrange chicken breasts over rice mixture. Pour Italian dressing over chicken.

Cover and bake at 400 degrees F for 30 minutes. Place vegetables around chicken. Bake uncovered 20 to 25 minutes. Top chicken with 1/2 cup French fried onions and bake for 5 minutes. Yield: 4 servings.

Chicken and Macaroni Casserole

1 1/2 cups cooked chicken, cut into bite-size pieces
1 1/2 cups uncooked elbow macaroni
1 cup shredded cheddar cheese
1 (4 oz.) can mushroom pieces, drained
1/4 cup chopped pimiento
1 (10.5 oz.) can cream of chicken or celery soup
1 cup milk
1/2 teaspoon salt
1/2 teaspoon curry powder, if desired

In a bowl, combine all ingredients. Pour in an ungreased 2-quart baking dish. Cover; bake for 1 hour at 350 degrees F. Yield: 4 servings.

Chicken Chasseur

8-10 boneless, skinless chicken breast halves
Salt
1/2 cup flour
6 tablespoons butter
6 tablespoons olive oil
1 medium onion, finely chopped
1 lb. mushrooms, sliced thin
1 cup white wine
1 jigger brandy
1 cup tomato sauce
1/2 cup canned chicken broth
1 tablespoon Kitchen Bouquet browning and seasoning sauce
Juice of 1 lemon
4 tablespoons fresh parsley, chopped

Lightly sprinkle salt on chicken and dredge in flour. Brown in a mixture of butter and olive oil for about 8 minutes, 4 minutes on each side. Transfer to casserole dish and sauté onions until transparent. Add mushrooms to onions, sauté for a few minutes, then add wine, brandy, tomato sauce, chicken broth, Kitchen Bouquet and lemon juice. Bring sauce to a quick boil, stirring all the while; pour over chicken.

Bake at 325 degrees F for 45 minutes covered, then 30 minutes uncovered. Baste two or three times during uncovered cooking. Sprinkle with fresh chopped parsley. Yield: 8 servings.

Low-Fat Chicken Cordon Bleu

4 boneless, skinless chicken breast halves
4 thin 1/2 oz. slices of reduced fat ham
2 tablespoons skim milk
1/4 cup crushed cornflakes
4 thin 1/2 oz. slices of reduced fat Swiss cheese

Preheat oven to 400 degrees F. Cut pocket in center of each chicken breast and tuck a slice of ham inside; roll in milk, then in crushed cornflakes. Arrange in 8x8" baking pan coated with nonstick cooking spray. Bake 25 minutes at 400 degrees F, then top each with a slice of cheese. Bake until cheese melts. Yield: 4 servings.

Chicken-Corn Casserole

6 cups cooked chicken, diced
1 large package noodles or macaroni
1 (4 oz.) can mushrooms
1 (4 oz.) jar pimientos
1 (15.25 oz.) can whole kernel corn

Cheese Sauce:
1 tablespoon flour
2 tablespoons margarine
2 cups milk
1 lb. Velveeta cheese, diced
Salt and pepper

Combine chicken, noodles, mushrooms, pimientos and corn. Mix cheese sauce ingredients together and add to chicken mixture. Pour into an ungreased casserole dish and bake at 350 degrees F for 1 hour. Yield: 3 to 4 servings.

Chicken-Tomato Pizza

8 oz. boneless, skinless chicken breasts, cut in bite-size pieces
1/3 cup prepared pesto
1 medium onion, sliced thin
3 medium plum tomatoes, sliced thin
14-inch prepared pizza crust
2 cups shredded mozzarella cheese

Preheat oven to 450 degrees F. Spray a non-stick skillet with non-stick cooking spray; cook and stir chicken over medium heat for 2 minutes. Add pesto and onion; continue cooking for 3 minutes, stirring constantly. Place chicken mixture and tomato slices on pizza crust. Sprinkle cheese over toppings. Bake 8 minutes at 450 degrees F or until pizza is hot and cheese is melted. Yield: 6 servings.

Cheesy Chicken

3 to 4 cups cooked chicken, cut up
2 large onions, chopped
1 large green pepper, chopped
1/2 cup margarine
10 oz. package spaghetti, cooked
1 (14.5 oz.) can diced tomatoes
1 lb. Velveeta cheese
1 (8.5 oz.) can English peas (tiny) or chopped broccoli
1 (4.5 oz.) can sliced mushrooms
Salt and pepper to taste

Sauté onion and peppers in margarine. Add mixture to cooked spaghetti. Mix tomatoes, cheese, peas or broccoli and mushrooms and add to spaghetti, stirring until cheese is melted. Sprinkle with salt and pepper to taste. Pour mixture into two large casserole dishes and bake at 350 degrees F for 15 to 20 minutes. Yield: 6 servings.

Monterey Jack Chicken

3 cups chopped, cooked chicken
1/2 cup cottage cheese
3 oz. cream cheese, softened
1/2 cup sour cream
1 (10.5 oz.) can cream of chicken soup
1 teaspoon salt
1/8 teaspoon garlic powder
1 (4 oz.) can chopped green chiles, drained
3 cups cooked rice
1 cup shredded Monterey Jack cheese
2 tomatoes, chopped
3/4 cup corn chips, crumbled

Combine the cottage cheese, cream cheese and sour cream in a medium bowl and mix well. In a large bowl, mix together the soup, salt, garlic powder, chicken, green chiles, rice, cheese and tomatoes. Stir the cottage cheese mixture into the chicken mixture. Spoon into a greased 13x9-inch baking dish. Sprinkle the top with corn chips. Bake, uncovered, at 350 degrees F for 30 minutes or until browned and bubbly. Yield: 6 to 8 servings.

Chicken and Rolls Casserole

4 cups cooked chicken, cubed
1 (10.5 oz.) can cream of chicken soup
1 (10.5 oz.) can cream of celery soup
1 (8 oz.) can water chestnuts, drained & sliced
1 (4 oz.) can mushroom stems & pieces, drained
2/3 cup mayonnaise or salad dressing
1/2 cup sour cream
1/2 cup chopped onion
1/2 cup chopped celery
1 (8 oz.) can refrigerated crescent rolls
6 oz. shredded Swiss or American cheese
2 to 4 tablespoons margarine, melted

In a large bowl, combine chicken, soups, water chestnuts, mushrooms, mayonnaise, sour cream, onion and celery. Pour into a large saucepan, and cook over medium heat until hot and bubbly.

Pour into ungreased 13x9-inch baking dish. Place rolls over chicken mixture. Mix together cheese and melted margarine and spread on rolls. Bake at 350 degrees F for 25 minutes, or until top is golden brown. Yield: 4 servings.

Crunchy Chicken

2 cups cooked, diced chicken
1 (10.5 oz.) can cream of chicken soup
1 teaspoon lemon juice
1/2 teaspoon salt
3/4 cup Miracle Whip Free
1 cup drained, sliced water chestnuts
1/2 cup celery, diced
3 teaspoons minced onion
2 cups cooked brown rice
2 tablespoons margarine
1 cup cornflakes, crushed
1/2 cup almonds, sliced

In a large bowl, combine chicken, soup, lemon juice, salt, Miracle Whip, water chestnuts, celery, onion and rice. Put mixture into a 2 quart baking dish. Melt margarine; add cornflakes and almonds. Sprinkle cornflake mixture on top of chicken. Bake at 375 degrees F for 25 minutes. Yield: 3 servings.

Chicken - Chile Casserole

4 to 6 boneless, skinless chicken breast halves, cooked and cubed
1 (10.5 oz.) can cream of mushroom soup
1 (10.5 oz.) can cream of chicken soup
1 small onion
1 cup milk
Salt and pepper to taste
1 package corn tortillas, cut in quarters
1 (4 oz.) can whole green chilies
1 lb. cheddar cheese, grated

In a bowl, make a sauce by combining mushroom soup, chicken soup, onion, milk, salt and pepper.

Grease a casserole dish. Layer in dish - 1/2 of the quartered corn tortillas; 1/2 of the cooked chicken, cubed; 1/2 of the green chilies, 1/2 of the sauce (soup mixture); 1/2 of the grated cheese. Repeat. Bake at 350 degrees F for 1 hour covered, then 15 minutes uncovered. Yield: 4 servings.

Coconut Chicken Breasts

4 boneless, skinless chicken breast halves
1/2 cup sweetened condensed milk
2 tablespoons spicy brown mustard
2/3 cup Bisquick
2/3 cup coconut
1/2 teaspoon paprika
1/4 cup melted butter

In a bowl, mix condensed milk and mustard together. In another bowl, combine Bisquick, coconut and paprika. Dip chicken in milk coating mixture and then roll in coconut coating. Place the coated chicken breasts into a casserole dish and drizzle melted butter over them. Bake, covered, at 375 degrees F for 40 minutes. Yield: 4 servings.

Chicken and 3 Cheese French Bread Pizza

1/2 cup butter or margarine, softened
1/3 cup grated Parmesan cheese
1/2 cup (2 oz.) shredded Cheddar cheese
1/4 teaspoon dried Italian seasoning
1 clove garlic, pressed
1 (16 oz.) loaf French bread, sliced
1 (10 oz.) can white chicken chunks, drained and flaked
1 cup (4 oz.) shredded Mozzarella cheese
1/4 cup green onions, chopped
1/4 cup bell pepper, chopped

In a small bowl, combine butter or margarine, Parmesan cheese, Cheddar cheese, Italian seasoning and garlic. Spread the mixture evenly on the bread. Add chicken on top. On top of chicken, add Mozzarella cheese, onions and peppers. Bake at 350 degrees F for 10 minutes or until cheese melts. Yield: 2 to 3 servings.

Easy Chicken Casserole

4 cups diced cooked chicken
3 hard-cooked eggs, coarsely chopped
1 (14.5 oz.) can French style green beans, drained
1 (8 oz.) can water chestnuts, diced
1 (4 oz.) jar sliced pimientos, drained
1 1/2 cups cooked rice
1 cup celery, chopped
1 cup slivered almonds
3 tablespoons butter or margarine
1 large onion, chopped
2 (10.5 oz.) cans cream of mushroom soup, undiluted
1 cup sliced fresh mushrooms
1 cup mayonnaise
1 teaspoon pepper
1 teaspoon paprika
1 (4 oz.) can potato sticks

Preheat oven to 350 degrees F. Lightly grease a 3-quart casserole dish; set aside. Combine chicken, eggs, green beans, water chestnuts, pimientos, rice, celery, and almonds; set aside.

Melt margarine in small skillet over medium-high heat. Add onion and sauté 4 to 5 minutes until tender. Add soup, mushrooms, mayonnaise, and pepper. Stir until well mixed. Pour over chicken mixture and stir. Spoon into prepared casserole dish. Sprinkle with paprika and top with potato sticks. Bake 40 minutes until heated through and bubbly. Yield: 4 servings.

Chicken Chip Casserole

2 cups chopped cooked chicken
1/2 cup chopped pecans
2 teaspoons dried minced onion
2 cups sliced celery
1 cup mayonnaise
2 teaspoons lemon juice
1/2 cup cheddar cheese, shredded
1 cup potato chips, broken

Combine chicken, pecans, onion, celery, mayonnaise and lemon juice. Place in a greased 1-1/2 qt. casserole dish. Combine cheese and chips. Sprinkle on top. Bake, uncovered, at 375 degrees F for 30 minutes or until heated. Yield: 4 servings.

Chicken Macaroni Bake

2 cups cooked chicken, diced
3 cups cooked elbow macaroni
2 1/2 cups canned apple slices
2 cups Cheddar or American cheese, grated
1 small onion, chopped
2 tablespoons butter or margarine
2 cups tomato sauce
1/4 teaspoon basil
1/4 teaspoon salt

Combine 1 1/2 cups apple slices, chicken and macaroni in a 9 x 9-inch casserole dish. Mix in 1 cup Cheddar cheese. Cook onion in butter, then add tomato sauce, basil and salt. Mix into ingredients in casserole dish. Top with remaining Cheddar cheese and apple slices. Cover and bake at 375 degrees F for 45 minutes. Yield: 4 servings.

Filled Chicken Breasts

4 (6 oz.) boneless, skinless chicken breast halves
1 (8 oz.) container garlic & herb spreadable cheese
1/4 cup buttermilk
2 egg whites
1/2 cup cracker crumbs
1/2 cup Italian seasoned bread crumbs
1/8 teaspoon pepper
1/8 teaspoon salt
1 tablespoon olive oil

Preheat oven to 400 degrees F. Flatten each chicken breast by pounding with a rolling pin or mallet. On one side of each chicken breast, spread the garlic & herb cheese. Fold short ends of each chicken breast over center, covering cheese, and secure with toothpicks.

In a small bowl, combine buttermilk and egg whites. Combine cracker crumbs, breadcrumbs, salt and pepper in a shallow dish. Dip each breast into buttermilk mixture, then in bread crumbs.

Cook chicken in hot olive oil in a large non-stick skillet for 5 minutes on each side or until breasts are browned. Place a wire rack on a cookie sheet and add the chicken to the wire rack. Bake at 400 degrees F for 20 minutes or until chicken is thoroughly cooked and no longer pink inside. Yield: 4 servings.

Chicken Spaghetti Dish

2 1/2 cups cooked chicken, cut up
1 (8 oz.) package spaghetti
4 tablespoons margarine
7 tablespoons flour
1 qt. chicken broth
3/4 lb. (3 cups) grated sharp cheddar cheese
1 (2 1/2 oz.) jar pimento, cut fine
1 green pepper, cut fine

Cook spaghetti according to package directions. Remove from heat and drain. Set aside. In a saucepan, combine margarine, flour and chicken broth. Cook over medium heat until thick. Mix with spaghetti; add 2 1/2 cups cheddar cheese, pimento and green pepper.

Place in greased casserole dish. Bake at 325 degrees F for 1 1/2 hours. Sprinkle 1/2 cup cheddar cheese on top the last half hour of baking. Yield: 4 to 5 servings.

Bombay Chicken

4 boneless, skinless chicken breast halves
1 (6 oz.) package dried mixed fruit or 3/4 cup raisins
1 cup rice
1/2 cup onion, chopped
2 teaspoons curry powder, divided
2 cups water
1 1/2 teaspoons sugar
1 teaspoon salt
2 tablespoons melted butter
1/2 teaspoon paprika

Combine fruit or raisins, rice, onion, 1 teaspoon curry, water, sugar, and salt in a casserole dish. Stir well. Add chicken on top of rice mixture. Combine 1 teaspoon curry, butter, paprika and brush mixture on chicken. Cover tightly with foil. Bake at 375 degrees F for 1 hour or until chicken is tender and liquid is absorbed. Yield: 3 to 4 servings.

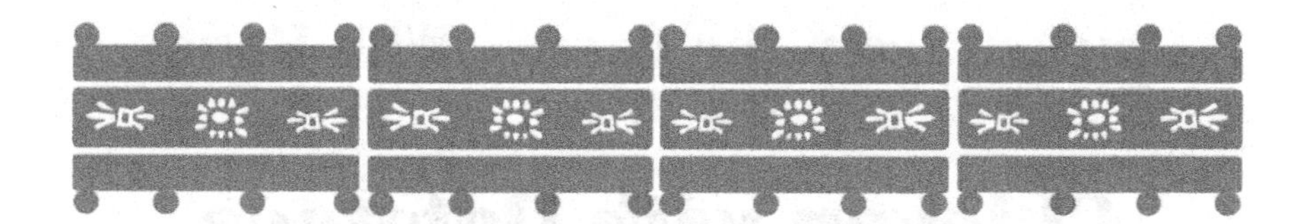

Bone-in Chicken from the Oven

Chicken from the Oven – With Bones

Chicken with Potatoes

6 bone-in chicken breast halves
4 tablespoons olive oil
2 cloves garlic, split
1/8 teaspoon salt
1/8 teaspoon pepper
2 onions, chopped
4 medium-sized potatoes, peeled and cut into 1/4 inch slices
2 bay leaves
1 tablespoon rosemary, crumbled
1 1/2 cups hot water, in which 2 chicken bouillon cubes have been dissolved
1/4 cup chopped parsley

In a skillet, heat the olive oil, then cook the garlic in the oil until brown; remove and discard the garlic. In the hot oil, cook the chicken until it is well browned and partially done (about 20 minutes); season with salt and pepper. Remove chicken and set aside.

In the remaining oil, cook the onion and potatoes, stirring, until the onion is translucent. Add the bay leaves and rosemary. Pour onion and potatoes into a casserole dish. Add the chicken on top. Over the contents of the casserole dish, pour the bouillon. Bake, covered, at 350 degrees F for 45 minutes, or until the potatoes are very tender. Garnish with parsley. Yield: 6 servings.

Vanilla and Tarragon Baked Chicken

2 bone-in chicken breast halves with skin
3 to 6 fresh tarragon sprigs
Salt and pepper to taste
2 tablespoons chicken broth
1 tablespoon pure vanilla extract

Preheat oven to 350 degrees F. Line small baking pan with aluminum foil. Rinse chicken breasts; pat dry. Place in baking pan. Loosen skin gently with fingers. Place tarragon sprig under skin of each chicken breast. Sprinkle remaining tarragon over top. Season with salt and pepper.

Mix broth and vanilla in small bowl. Pour over chicken breasts. Seal chicken breasts securely in foil. Bake for 45 minutes, basting twice during baking. Drizzle basting liquid over chicken breasts; let stand for 5 to 10 minutes. Yield: 2 servings.

Honey Mustard Chicken and Vegetables

4 bone-in chicken breast halves with skin
1/2 cup honey
1/4 cup prepared mustard
1/4 cup butter or margarine
2 tablespoons finely chopped onion
2 tablespoons water
1 clove garlic, minced
2 teaspoons curry powder
1 teaspoon salt
1/4 teaspoon crushed red pepper
1/4 teaspoon ground ginger
Cooking oil or melted butter
4 large potatoes, peeled and quartered
6 medium carrots, cut into 1/2 inch pieces
2 medium apples, cored and cut into wedges

In a small saucepan, combine honey, mustard, butter or margarine, onion, water, garlic, curry powder, salt, pepper and ginger. Bring to boil, stirring constantly. Remove from heat; set aside.

Place potatoes, carrots and apples in the bottom of a baking dish. Place chicken breasts on top and baste with oil or butter. Pour most of the honey mixture over the chicken and vegetables. Cover and bake at 350 degrees F for approximately 1 hour or until tender. Baste occasionally with remaining honey mixture. Yield: 4 servings.

Mushroom Chicken

3 1/2 lbs. chicken pieces
1/4 cup flour
1/4 cup butter, melted
10 small onions, cooked
1/4 lb. mushrooms, sliced
2/3 cup evaporated milk, undiluted
1 (10.5 oz.) can cream of mushroom soup
1 cup American cheese, grated
1/4 cup fresh parsley, chopped, or 2 tablespoons dried parsley
3/4 teaspoon salt
1/8 teaspoon pepper
1/8 teaspoon paprika

Dip the chicken in flour. Place chicken, skin-side down, in melted butter in a shallow, 2-quart baking dish. Bake, uncovered, in at 425 degrees F for 30 minutes. Turn chicken; bake 15 to 20 minutes longer, or until tender. Turn oven down to 325 degrees F.

Meanwhile, in a medium saucepan, combine the remaining ingredients (except paprika) and heat over medium heat until cheese is melted and sauce is thoroughly heated. Pour off excess fat from chicken, then pour cheese sauce over chicken. Sprinkle with paprika. Cover baking dish with aluminum foil. Bake at 325 degrees F for 15 to 20 minutes. Yield: 6 to 8 servings.

Princess Kaiulani Chicken

1 (2 1/2 to 3 1/2-lb.) chicken pieces, bone-in, skinned
1 medium onion
1 (20 oz.) can crushed pineapple
1 cup ketchup
2 tablespoons Worcestershire sauce
2 tablespoons prepared mustard
2 tablespoons vinegar

Place chicken, skin side up, in a 13x9-inch baking dish. Mix together onion, pineapple, ketchup, Worcestershire sauce, mustard and vinegar in a saucepan. Simmer 5 minutes. Pour over chicken. Bake at 350 degrees F for 1 hour or until chicken is tender. Yield: 4 to 5 servings.

Oven Barbecued Chicken

1 (2 1/2 to 3-lb.) whole chicken, cut into pieces
3 tablespoons brown sugar
2 tablespoons Worcestershire sauce
2 tablespoons water
2 tablespoons butter (melted)
2 tablespoons vinegar
2 tablespoons ketchup
1 tablespoon lemon juice
1 teaspoon chili powder
1 teaspoon sugar
1 teaspoon paprika
1 teaspoon mustard
1 teaspoon salt

Mix all ingredients together, except chicken, in a saucepan. Bring to a boil over medium heat, stirring frequently. Remove from heat.

Dip chicken in mixture; put in a greased baking dish. Pour remainder of mixture over chicken. Bake, covered, at 350 degrees F for 2 hours, basting occasionally. Uncover 20 minutes before chicken is done. Yield: 4 servings.

Polynesian Chicken

6 chicken pieces, bone-in
1/2 cup bottled French dressing
1/2 cup chicken broth
2 tablespoons soy sauce
3 tablespoons lemon juice
1 tablespoon cornstarch
1 (20 oz.). can chunk pineapple
1 (7 oz.) package pea pods
1 (8 oz.) can water chestnuts, drained and sliced
Hot cooked rice

Brush chicken with French dressing. Sprinkle with salt and pepper and arrange in a baking dish. Brown in 450 degrees oven uncovered. Combine chicken broth, soy sauce and lemon juice, gradually adding cornstarch. Pour over chicken.

Bake at 350 degrees F until chicken is tender. Top with pineapple, pea pods and water chestnuts and heat until warm. Serve with hot cooked rice. Yield: 2 to 3 servings.

Lemon Chicken

6 to 8 chicken pieces, bone-in
2 lemons
1/3 cup flour
1/2 teaspoon paprika
1 1/2 teaspoons salt
4 tablespoons vegetable oil or olive oil
2 tablespoons brown sugar
1 cup chicken broth

Cut one lemon in thin slices. Grate peel from 2nd lemon and set grated peel aside; cut the grated lemon in half and squeeze the juice over the chicken.

Shake chicken in a paper bag with the flour, paprika and salt. Heat oil in a skillet. Add chicken and brown slowly in oil, about 4 minutes per side. Place chicken in a casserole dish. Sprinkle grated lemon peel over the chicken. Sprinkle brown sugar over chicken then cover chicken with sliced lemon. Add the broth to the casserole dish. Cover and bake at 350 degrees F until chicken is tender, 40 to 45 minutes. Yield: 4 to 6 servings.

Roasted Curried Mango Chicken

4 lb. whole chicken
1/4 fresh lemon or lime juice
3/4 teaspoon salt
1 clove garlic, minced
2 teaspoons curry
1 ripe mango, pitted and peeled
4 ripe mangos, pitted and sliced in half lengthwise
6 medium onions, blanched with skins on
3 tablespoons butter
1 tablespoon flour

Preheat oven to 350 degrees F. Spray a roasting pan with non-stick cooking spray. Rinse and pat dry chicken. Sprinkle chicken inside and out with lemon or lime juice. Rub with salt and garlic. Brush chicken with curry. Stuff 1 mango - pitted and peeled, in cavity. Arranged rest of mangos (cut side down) and onions, around chicken.

Dot chicken with butter and bake at 350 degrees F for 1 hour 45 minutes, basting occasionally. Add 1/4 cup water to pan and bake an additional 15 minutes. Take chicken and vegetables out. Take skin off onions and mangos. Optional - Make gravy from drippings with a little water and flour. Yield: 6 to 8 servings.

Sesame Chicken

2 (2 1/2 to 3-lb.) chickens, cut into pieces
2 cups instant potato flakes
1/2 cup sesame seeds
2 tablespoons parsley
2 teaspoons salt
2/3 cup butter, melted
1/2 teaspoon tarragon
2 tablespoons lemon juice

Combine potatoes flakes, sesame seeds, parsley and salt. Melt butter and tarragon, add lemon juice. Dip chicken in butter mixture. Roll in potato flake mixture. Place on large baking sheet. Bake at 350 degrees F for 1 1/2 hours. Yield: 6 to 8 servings.

Manhattan Chicken

5 to 6 lbs. of chicken pieces
4 tablespoons margarine
3 tablespoons sherry or white wine
1 (32 oz.) can peach halves in heavy syrup (reserve 1/2 cup syrup)
1 cup barbecue sauce
1/8 teaspoon garlic powder
1 tablespoon lemon juice
1 (3 or 4 oz.) can or jar onions

Brown chicken in margarine for about 8 minutes, 4 minutes on each side. Remove from pan. Add sherry to drippings. Cook down to one half amount. Add 1/2 cup peach syrup, barbecue sauce, garlic powder and lemon juice.

Arrange chicken in casserole dish and cover with sauce. Arrange peach halves and drained onions over chicken. Bake uncovered at 325 degrees F for one hour. Baste every 15 minutes. Yield: 6 to 8 servings.

Teriyaki Chicken

4 to 6 bone-in chicken breasts halves
1 tablespoon cornstarch
1 tablespoon cold water
1/2 cup sugar
1/2 cup soy sauce
1/4 cup vinegar
1/8 teaspoon garlic powder
1/2 teaspoon ginger
1/4 teaspoon pepper

In a saucepan, combine cornstarch, water, sugar, soy sauce, vinegar, garlic, ginger and pepper. Heat over medium heat until sauce is thickened. Place chicken in 13x9-inch baking dish; brush with glaze.

Bake at 425 degrees F for 30 minutes, brushing with glaze every 10 minutes. Then turn chicken over and bake another 20 minutes after brushing with glaze. Yield: 4 servings.

Easy Oven Chicken

1 (2 1/2 to 3 lb.) chicken, cut into pieces
1 cup sour cream
1 teaspoon Worcestershire sauce
1 teaspoon lemon juice
1 teaspoon celery salt
1 teaspoon paprika
1/2 teaspoon salt
1/4 teaspoon pepper
1 cup fine dry bread crumbs
1/3 cup margarine, melted

Mix together sour cream, Worcestershire sauce, lemon juice, celery salt, paprika, salt and pepper. Dip chicken in sour cream mixture; roll in bread crumbs; pour melted margarine in a baking dish and place chicken skin side up in the margarine. Bake for 1 hour at 375 degrees F. Yield: 4 servings.

Honey Glazed Chicken

1 (3-lb.) whole chicken, cut into pieces
1/2 cup flour
1 teaspoon salt
1/2 teaspoon cayenne pepper
1/2 cup margarine, melted
1/4 cup lemon juice
1/4 cup honey
1/4 cup brown sugar, packed
1 tablespoon soy sauce
1 1/2 teaspoons curry powder

Mix flour, salt and pepper together in a large resealable plastic bag. Add the chicken pieces; seal and shake to coat. Pour half the margarine into a 13x9-inch baking pan. Place the coated chicken in the pan. Bake, uncovered, at 350 degrees F for 30 minutes.

Combine the lemon juice, honey, brown sugar, soy sauce, curry powder and remaining 1/4 cup margarine in a saucepan over medium heat. Heat until the brown sugar is dissolved, stirring constantly. Remove from the heat and pour evenly over the chicken. Bake for 45 minutes longer, removing from the oven every 15 minutes to baste the chicken with the pan drippings. Yield: 6 servings.

Galetto Marinara

1 (3 to 3 1/2-lb.) chicken pieces
1/4 cup margarine
Salt and pepper
1/8 teaspoon flour
1/2 teaspoon dill weed
1 3/4 cups Marinara sauce (recipe below)
1/3 cup grated Parmesan cheese

Melt margarine in 9" x 13" x 2" pan. Sprinkle salt, pepper and flour lightly on chicken. Place chicken, skin side up, in pan. Bake at 450 degrees F for 30 to 40 minutes. Combine marinara sauce with dill and spoon over chicken. Top with cheese. Bake at 350 for 30 minutes longer. Yield: 4 servings.

Marinara Sauce:
1 minced garlic clove
1/4 cup chopped onion
2 tablespoons oil
1 2/3 cups tomato puree
1 teaspoon salt
1/2 teaspoon oregano
1/4 tablespoon basil
1/8 teaspoon pepper
2 teaspoons chopped parsley

Sauté garlic clove, onion in oil. Add tomato puree, salt, oregano, basil, pepper and parsley. Simmer uncovered for 15 minutes.

Barbecued Chicken in Foil

1 (2 lb.) chicken, cut into pieces
1/4 cup water
3 tablespoons ketchup
2 tablespoons Worcestershire sauce
2 tablespoons margarine or butter, melted
2 tablespoons vinegar
1 tablespoon lemon juice
2 teaspoons chili powder
2 teaspoons salt
1 teaspoon paprika
1 teaspoon dry mustard
1/4 teaspoon red pepper

Mix together all ingredients except chicken. Dip the chicken pieces in the sauce and place in a single layer on a large sheet of aluminum foil (18 to 24"). Pour any remaining sauce over the top of the chicken. Tightly seal foil and place on a rack in a roasting pan.

Bake at 500 degrees F for 15 minutes. Reduce heat to 350 degrees F and continue to bake for 1 1/4 to 1 1/2 hours, or until the chicken is tender and cooked through. Yield: 4 servings.

Chicken Marengo

2 1/2 to 3 1/2-lb. chicken pieces, skinned
1 teaspoon salt
1/2 teaspoon paprika
2 tablespoons oil
1 (4 oz.) can mushrooms (reserve liquid)
1 medium onion, chopped
1 green pepper, chopped
2 ribs celery, chopped
4 cups canned or fresh tomatoes
Garlic salt, to taste

Sprinkle chicken with salt and paprika. Brown in hot oil in skillet for about 8 minutes, 4 minutes on each side. Remove chicken. Drain liquid from mushrooms into skillet. Add onions, pepper, celery and garlic. Cover and cook a few minutes. Add the tomatoes.

Place in a large baking dish with the chicken and cover with aluminum foil. Bake at 325 degrees F for at least 1 hour or until chicken is cooked through. Yield: 4 servings.

Chicken Country Captain

3 to 3 1/2-lb. chicken pieces
6 slices bacon
Salt and pepper to taste
1/2 cup flour
1 cup cooked rice
2 tablespoons butter
1 onion, sliced
1 large green pepper, sliced
1 teaspoon salt
1/4 teaspoon pepper
1 clove garlic, minced
1 (28 oz.) can tomatoes
1 teaspoon curry powder
1 teaspoon chopped parsley
1/4 teaspoon oregano
1/4 lb. roasted almonds, sliced

Fry bacon until crisp in large skillet. Remove bacon from pan; leave bacon drippings in pan. Combine salt and pepper to taste with flour; dip chicken in flour mixture. Brown chicken in bacon drippings in skillet for 10 to 15 minutes. Remove chicken from pan. Place in large greased casserole dish. Combine with rice.

Discard bacon drippings. Add butter to skillet and sauté onion and green pepper. Add 1 teaspoon salt, 1/4 teaspoon pepper, garlic, tomatoes, curry powder, parsley, oregano and almonds. Cook for 15 minutes until well blended. Pour sauce over rice. Bake 45 to 60 minutes at 350 degrees F. Top with bacon. Makes 4 to 6 servings.

Chicken with Sausage

1 (2 1/2 to 3-lb.) whole chicken, cut into pieces
1 lb. sweet Italian sausage links, cut up
6 medium potatoes, peeled and quartered
1 teaspoon paprika
1 teaspoon oregano
1 teaspoon salt
1/2 teaspoon pepper
1/2 teaspoon garlic powder
1/4 cup vegetable oil

Preheat the oven to 425 degrees F. Arrange the potatoes in a large baking dish. Mix the paprika, oregano, salt, pepper and garlic powder and sprinkle half the mixture over the potatoes. Add the sausage and chicken on top of potatoes. Pour the vegetable oil over the chicken and sausage; sprinkle with the remaining seasonings.

Bake, covered, at 425 degrees F for 1 hour. Uncover and bake at 375 degrees F for 30 minutes, or until the chicken turns a golden brown color. Yield: 4 to 6 servings.

Honey Mustard Chicken

4 bone-in chicken breasts, skin removed
1 medium red onion, cut into 8 wedges
1 medium butternut squash, peeled, cut into 1-inch cubes (4 cups)
3/4 cup honey mustard dressing
1/2 teaspoon dried rosemary leaves, crushed
1/2 teaspoon salt
1/4 teaspoon garlic powder
2 cups frozen sugar snap peas

Preheat oven to 425 degrees F. Spray a roasting pan with non-stick cooking spray. Place chicken in pan; add onion and squash around chicken. In a small bowl, make sauce by mixing honey mustard dressing, rosemary, salt and garlic powder. Brush chicken, onion and squash with half of the sauce. Bake, uncovered, at 425 degrees F for 20 minutes.

Remove pan from the oven. Stir in snap peas. Brush vegetables and chicken with the other half of sauce. Return to oven; bake 25 minutes longer, or until vegetables are tender. Yield: 4 servings.

Chicken with Cheese Sauce

6 to 8 bone-in chicken breast halves
2 tablespoons margarine
2 tablespoons oil
Salt and pepper, to taste
2 tablespoons margarine
1 onion, chopped
1 clove garlic, crushed
2 tablespoons flour
2 teaspoons paprika
2 cups warm milk
1 cup grated Gruyere cheese

In a skillet, heat the margarine and oil; add the chicken to the skillet and sprinkle with salt and pepper. Cook until browned for about 8 minutes, 4 minutes on each side. Remove chicken to a baking dish.

Add the margarine and onion to the fat in the skillet, and cook until onion is translucent. Add garlic, flour and paprika. Gradually add the milk, stirring the mixture until it is thick and smooth. Add the cheese, stirring until the cheese is melted. Pour the sauce over the chicken.

Bake, covered, at 350 degrees F for 1 hour, or until chicken is tender. Yield: 6 servings.

Note: to crush a clove of garlic without a press, wrap the garlic clove in a paper towel. Use a soup can to crush it and the skin should come right off.

Euskara Chicken

1 (3-lb.) chicken, cut into pieces, skin removed
1/4 lb. fresh mushrooms, thinly sliced
1 large green pepper, cut in strips
2 medium onions, thinly sliced and separated into rings

2 cloves garlic, minced
1/2 teaspoon salt
1/4 teaspoon pepper
1/4 teaspoon cayenne pepper
1 cup tomato puree
1/4 cup chicken broth
2 teaspoons cornstarch
1 tablespoon water

Preheat oven to 375 degrees F. Place mushrooms, green pepper and onions in a roasting pan. Add chicken pieces on top of vegetables; sprinkle with garlic, salt, pepper and cayenne pepper.

In a separate bowl, mix tomato puree and chicken broth; add to roasting pan. Bake uncovered for 1 hour or until chicken and vegetables are tender and brown. Remove from oven and pour liquid into a skillet. Mix cornstarch and water; stir into skillet. Bring to a boil, stirring constantly until thickened. Place chicken and vegetables on a serving platter. Pour sauce over chicken. Yield: 4 servings.

Currant and Apricot Chicken

2 chickens (2 1/2 to 3 lbs. each), quartered
1/3 cup apple juice
1/3 cup fresh orange juice
1 1/2 cups orange marmalade
Salt and pepper, to taste
1 teaspoon ground ginger
8 oz. dried currants
8 oz. dried apricots
1/4 cup brown sugar

Preheat oven to 375 degrees F. Place the chicken pieces, skin side up, in a shallow roasting pan. Pour the apple and orange juice over the chicken then spread marmalade on chicken. Sprinkle generously with salt, pepper and ginger. Bake 20 minutes at 375 degrees F.

Remove from oven and add the currants and apricots to the pan. Sprinkle the fruit with the brown sugar and return to the oven. Bake, basting frequently, until the chicken is browned, 40 to 45 minutes. Serve with juices from pan as gravy. Yield: 6 to 8 servings.

Irish Chicken

6 bone-in chicken breast halves, skin removed
1 cup dry white wine
1 teaspoon dried whole oregano
1 teaspoon dried whole basil
1/2 teaspoon garlic powder
1/4 teaspoon salt
1/8 teaspoon pepper
2 tablespoons butter or margarine, melted
1 (14 oz.) jar sweet cherry peppers, undrained
1 lb. fresh mushrooms, halved

Preheat oven to 350 degrees F. Spray a 13x9-inch baking dish with non-stick cooking spray and add chicken. In a bowl, combine wine, oregano, basil, salt and pepper and garlic powder. Pour wine mixture over chicken. Marinate in refrigerator, covered, for 4 to 6 hours.

Brush butter or margarine on chicken; pour peppers and liquid over top. Cover and bake at 350 degrees F for 40 minutes. Add mushrooms. Bake, uncovered, an additional 20 minutes or until done. Yield: 6 servings.

Hawaiian Chicken

6 lbs. chicken pieces
3 tablespoons cornstarch
3 tablespoons water
1 1/2 cups sugar
1 1/2 cups soy sauce
3/4 cup vinegar
4 garlic cloves, minced
1 teaspoon ground ginger
1/2 teaspoon pepper
6 pineapple rings
Hot cooked rice

Broil chicken 10 minutes skin side down and then 10 minutes skin side up. In a saucepan, combine cornstarch in water then add sugar, soy sauce, vinegar, garlic, ground ginger, pepper. Cook, stirring until sauce thickens.

Place chicken halves, skin side up, in shallow casserole dish. Pour sauce over chicken and bake uncovered at 350 degrees F for 1 hour. Baste several times during baking. Garnish with pineapple rings. Serve over rice. Yield: 6 to 8 servings.

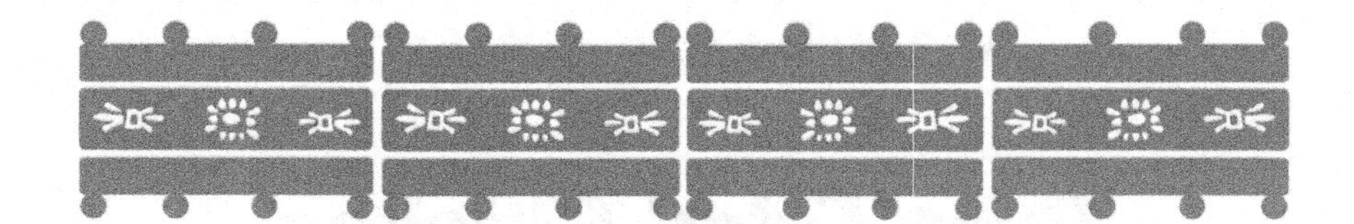

Spanish-Style Chicken

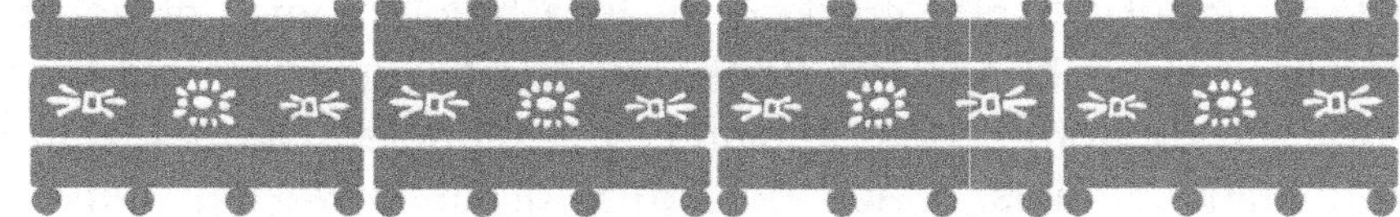

Spanish-Style Chicken

Oven Fried Chicken Chimichangas

1 lb. boneless, skinless chicken breasts, cooked and flaked
1 (4 oz.) can chopped green chilies, drained
2 cups shredded Monterey Jack cheese
1/2 cup green onions, sliced
1 package flour tortillas
1/4 cup vegetable oil
Shredded lettuce
Salsa
Sour cream

Preheat oven to 425 degrees F. Combine cooked chicken, green chilies, cheese and green onions. Microwave tortillas on high for 10 seconds or until warm. Brush both sides of tortilla with vegetable oil, keeping remaining tortillas warm.

Place about 1/2 cup chicken mixture below center of each tortilla. Fold right and left sides over the filling. Then fold the top and bottom sides, making a rectangle. Repeat with remaining tortillas. Place on lightly greased baking sheet. Bake at 425 degrees F for 10 minutes or until crisp and lightly brown. Serve with lettuce, salsa and sour cream. Yield: 4 servings.

Chicken Chalupa

4 large chicken breasts, cooked and diced
1 lb. sharp cheese - shredded
12 tortilla chips or corn chips
1 (10.5 oz.) can cream of chicken soup
1 (10.5 oz.) can cream of mushroom soup
1 small can diced green chilies
2/3 cup milk
1/2 cup sour cream
1 diced onion

Preheat oven to 350 degrees F. Grease a 13x9-inch baking dish. In a bowl, make a sauce by combining soups, chilies, milk, sour cream and onion. Layer the corn chips or tortilla chips (Break tortilla chips into bite size pieces.) in the bottom of dish. On top of chips, add diced chicken, sauce and cheese.

Cover dish with foil and bake for 45 minutes at 350 degrees F. Remove cover and bake for 15 additional minutes. Yield: 4 servings.

Easy Taquitos

1 1/2 cups chicken, cooked and shredded
12 corn tortillas
Cooking oil
Shredded lettuce
Tomato sauce
Sour cream

Wrap tortillas in damp paper towels. Microwave on high for 15 seconds or until warm. Wrap the tortillas in foil to keep warm. With a spoon, place a narrow row of filling along the center of each tortilla. Roll tortilla tightly and secure with a toothpick. While rolling the taquitos, heat about 1/4" of cooking oil to medium heat in a large, heavy skillet. Fry the taquitos, turning to brown evenly. Drain on paper towels. Serve garnished with lettuce, tomato sauce and cream to taste. Yield: 3 servings.

Tamale Pie

1 cup cooked chicken, cut fine
1/2 cup olive oil
1 large onion
1 can cream style corn
1 can tomato soup
1/2 lb. salt pork, ground
1 can minced ripe olives
2 eggs, well beaten
1 cup yellow corn meal
3/4 cup milk
1/2 teaspoon cayenne pepper
1/2 cup cheddar cheese, shredded

Brown onion in olive oil, add corn and tomato soup; cook for 5 minutes. Add salt pork and cook 5 minutes more. Beat eggs, milk, corn meal and cayenne pepper together. Add to mixture and cook 10 minutes. Add minced olives and meat. Put in buttered casserole dish. Bake at 325 degrees for 20 minutes. Sprinkle cheese on top and bake 5 minutes more. Yield: 4 servings.

Spicy Hot Jalapeno Chicken

2 1/2 lbs. boneless, skinless chicken breast halves, cooked and chopped
4 fresh jalapenos, seeded and diced
1 garlic clove, minced
1 onion, chopped
1 tablespoon vegetable oil
1/2 teaspoon cumin
1/2 teaspoon chili powder
1 (10 oz.) package frozen chopped spinach, thawed and squeezed dry
1 (10.5 oz.) can cream of chicken soup
1/2 teaspoon salt
2 cups sour cream
1 1/2 packages corn chips
2 cups (8 oz.) shredded Monterey Jack cheese

In a saucepan over medium-low heat, sauté the jalapenos, garlic and onion in the oil until tender. Stir in the cumin and chili powder and cook for 1 minute. Stir in spinach,
soup and salt; bring to a boil. Reduce the heat and cook, covered, for 5 minutes. Stir in the chicken and sour cream. Cook until heated through; do not boil.

Layer one-third of the com chips, one-third of the cheese and one-half of the chicken mixture in a greased 3-quart baking dish. Repeat the layers. Top with the remaining one-third of the com chips and one-third of the cheese. Bake at 350 degrees F for 30 to 40 minutes or until bubbly. Yield: 10 servings.

Chicken Enchiladas

6 to 8 boneless, skinless chicken breast halves
1 (4 1/2 oz.) can black olives, chopped
1 cup onion, chopped
1 cup Jack cheese
2 (10.5 oz.) cans cream of chicken soup
1/2 pint sour cream
1/2 cup green chilies
1 dozen flour tortillas
1 cup Cheddar cheese or Mexican blend, shredded
5 cherry tomatoes, sliced
2 green onions, coarsely chopped

Cook chicken; cut into bite-size pieces. In a bowl, mix chicken, olives, onion, and Jack cheese. Heat soup, sour cream and green chilies. Put half of soup mixture on bottom of 9x13-inch pan. Roll chicken mixture into the tortillas. Put filled tortillas in pan and pour rest of soup mixture on top. Spread with Cheddar or Mexican-blend cheese. Sprinkle with tomatoes and onions. Bake at 350 degrees F for 30 to 40 minutes. Yield: 4 servings.

Mexican Chicken Scoops

5 cups chopped, cooked chicken
2 cups (8 oz.) sharp Cheddar cheese, shredded
1 large red bell pepper, chopped
1/2 cup sliced black olives
3/4 cup chopped onion
1/2 cup sour cream
1/2 cup mayonnaise
3 (4 oz.) cans chopped green chiles, drained
1 envelope taco seasoning mix
Large sturdy corn chips for filling

Combine the chicken, cheese, bell pepper, olives, onion, sour cream, mayonnaise, chiles and taco seasoning mix in a bowl and mix well. Fill com chips with the chicken mixture and arrange on a baking sheet. Sprinkle with additional cheese. Broil until the cheese melts. Yield: 40 to 50 filled corn chips.

Chicken Tacos

6 to 8 bone-in chicken pieces, skinned
2 onions
2 garlic cloves
2 tablespoons lime juice
1/4 to 1/2 cup mayonnaise
1/2 teaspoon Tabasco sauce
Salt and pepper to taste
Lettuce
Tomato
Taco sauce
12 taco shells

Boil chicken with onions (chopped) and 2 whole garlic cloves. Shred chicken and add lime juice and mayonnaise, Tabasco sauce, salt and pepper to own taste (should make a soft paste). Place approximately 1 to 2 tablespoons chicken mixture in taco shells. Heat shells 10 to 12 minutes at 400 degrees F. Shred lettuce and squeeze lime juice onto lettuce. Slice tomato thin. While hot, top tacos with lettuce and tomato. Serve with taco sauce. Yield: 4 servings.

Chicken and Black Bean Enchiladas

3 cups chopped cooked chicken (can use rotisserie chicken)
1 (15 oz.) can black beans, rinsed and drained
1 (10 oz.) can diced tomatoes with green chiles
1 (8 3/4 oz.) can corn, drained
1 (8 oz.) package shredded Mexican four-cheese blend, divided
8 (8-inch) flour tortillas
2 (10 oz.) cans enchilada sauce

In a large bowl, combine chicken, beans, tomatoes and corn and 1 1/2 cup cheese. Spoon chicken mixture down the center of each tortilla, and roll up. Spray a 13x9-inch baking dish with non-stick cooking spray; place enchiladas, seam sides down, in baking dish.

Pour enchilada sauce over enchiladas; add remaining cheese on top. Bake, covered, at 350 degrees F for 20 minutes. Uncover and bake for 15 more minutes. Yield: 6 servings.

Easy Mexican Chicken

3 cups shredded chicken
8 corn tortillas, cut in 2 inch strips
2 (6 oz.) cans tomato sauce
1 (4 oz.) can diced green chilies
1 medium onion, chopped
1 (10.5 oz.) can cream of mushroom soup
1 (10.5 oz.) can cream of chicken soup
1 cup milk
2 cups (8 oz.) shredded cheddar cheese

Grease a 13x9-inch baking dish. Layer tortilla strips in bottom of dish. Cover with mixture of tomato sauce, diced chilies and onion. Spread chicken over tomato mixture. Cover with soups and milk. Sprinkle cheese over all. Bake at 350 degrees for 1 hour. Yield: 4 servings.

Chicken Flautas

1 cup cooked chicken, shredded
1 clove garlic, minced
1/4 cup onion, chopped
1 tablespoon vegetable oil
1 1/2 teaspoons cornstarch
1/4 cup chicken broth
1/2 teaspoon salt
1/4 teaspoon pepper
2 tablespoons chopped green chiles
6 (6-inch) corn tortillas
Vegetable oil
Guacamole

Sauté garlic and onion in oil in a skillet until tender. Combine chicken broth and cornstarch; add cornstarch mixture, chicken, salt, pepper and green chiles to onion mixture. Cook over medium heat, stirring constantly, until mixture thickens. Set aside.

Fry tortillas, one at a time, in 1/4 inch hot oil (375 degrees) about 6 seconds on each side. Drain on absorbent paper. Place 2 tablespoons chicken filling in center of each tortilla. Roll each tortilla tightly, and secure with a wooden toothpick. Heat oil in skillet. Add flautas, and brown on all sides over high heat (375 degrees). Drain on absorbent paper. Serve with guacamole. Yield: 2 servings.

Guacamole:
1 ripe avocado
2 tablespoons chopped onion
1 medium tomato, peeled and chopped
1 clove garlic, minced

2 tablespoons lemon juice
1/4 teaspoon salt
1/4 teaspoon pepper

Peel avocado, remove seeds and mash. Combine all ingredients in a small serving bowl, stirring until blended. Yield: 1 3/4 cups.

Spinach Chicken Enchiladas

4 boneless, skinless chicken breast halves, cut into thin strips
1/4 cup onion, chopped
1 (10 oz.) package frozen chopped spinach, thawed and drained
1 (10.5 oz.) can cream of mushroom soup
3/4 cup milk
1 cup sour cream
1 teaspoon onion powder
1 teaspoon nutmeg
1 teaspoon garlic powder
2 cups mozzarella cheese, shredded
8 (8-inch) flour tortillas

Cook onion and chicken in a large skillet over medium heat until chicken is cooked through and no longer pink inside. Remove from heat; add spinach and mix well.

In a bowl, make sauce by combining soup, milk, sour cream, onion powder, nutmeg and garlic powder; mix well. Stir in 3/4 cup of sauce into spinach and chicken mixture. Divide mixture among tortillas. Roll up and place seam side down, in a 13x9-inch greased pan. Pour the remaining sauce over enchiladas. Cover and bake at 350 degrees F for 30 minutes. Uncover and sprinkle with cheese; return to the oven for 10 to 15 minutes. Yield: 4 servings.

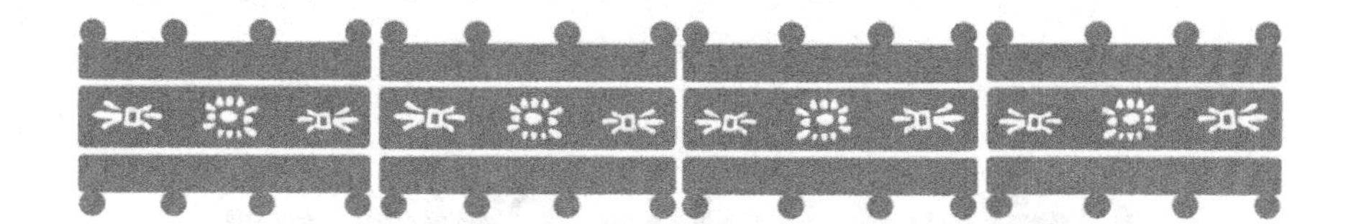

Grilled Chicken

Grilled Chicken

Grilled Salsa Chicken

1 (2 1/2 to 3-lb.) whole chicken, cut into quarters
Cayenne pepper
Pepper
Salt
1 (16 oz.) jar salsa (hot, medium, or mild)
1 (8 oz.) can tomato sauce
4 green onions, coarsely chopped

Arrange chicken pieces in an oblong baking dish (remove skin to reduce calories). Season with salt, pepper and cayenne pepper to taste. Combine salsa and tomato sauce and pour over chicken. Scatter chopped green onions over top. Cover with foil and bake at 350 degrees for 45 minutes.

Heat barbecue grill. Brush grill with oil to keep chicken from sticking. Remove chicken from oven. Carefully lift chicken pieces from sauce, reserving sauce for later use. Place chicken on hot grill and cook for 2 or 3 minutes on each side, or until nicely browned. Serve chicken and sauce with hot tortillas, rice, and tossed green salad. Yield: 4 servings.

Hawaiian Chicken Teriyaki

12 boneless, skinless chicken breast halves
3/4 cup brown sugar
3/4 cup soy sauce
1 clove fresh garlic, chopped
1 (1-inch) piece fresh ginger, crushed
1 tablespoon sesame oil
2 tablespoons sherry
1/2 bunch green onions, finely chopped
1 tablespoon roasted sesame seeds

Combine all ingredients, except chicken breasts, to make the marinade. Marinate chicken breasts for 2 to 4 hours in refrigerator. Grill chicken on barbecue until done. Yield: 12 servings.

Grilled Chicken Breasts

8 boneless, skinless chicken breast halves
2 cloves garlic (or 1/4 teaspoon garlic powder)
1 1/2 teaspoons salt
1/2 cup light brown sugar
3 tablespoons spicy brown mustard
3/4 cup cider vinegar
1 tablespoon lime juice
1 tablespoon lemon juice
6 tablespoons oil
1/8 teaspoon black pepper
1/8 teaspoon parsley

Mix all ingredients together (except chicken). Place chicken breasts in a shallow container and pour marinade over chicken. Marinate chicken breasts 8 hours in refrigerator. Grill over hot coals for 5 to 7 minutes on each side. Yield: 6 to 8 servings.

Afghanistan Chicken

4 lbs. bone-in chicken breasts and thighs, skin removed
1 cup plain low-fat yogurt
2 1/2 tablespoons lemon juice
1 tablespoon vegetable oil
1 teaspoon salt
1 garlic clove, crushed
1 teaspoon cumin
1 teaspoon ginger
1 teaspoon paprika
1 teaspoon almond extract

Mix all ingredients (except chicken) together. Reserve 1/8 cup marinade for basting and pour remainder of marinade over chicken. Marinate in refrigerator at least 1 hour. Grill chicken 6 to 8" above hot coals, basting and turning once. Grill time is 8 minutes a side and watch carefully so it doesn't dry out. Yield: 8 servings.

Apple Chicken Burgers

1 lb. ground chicken
1 medium apple
1/4 cup green onions, finely chopped
2 tablespoons apple juice
1 1/4 teaspoons poultry seasoning
1/2 teaspoon salt

Preheat grill. Chop the apple into small fine pieces. In a medium bowl, mix together apple, onions, apple juice, poultry seasoning and salt. Add ground chicken; combine well. Shape the mixture into 4 1/2-inch thick patties.

Spray grill with non-stick grilling spray or carefully oil the rack. Cook burgers over medium heat for 14 to 20 minutes or until patties are no longer pink in center, turning once. Yield: 4 servings.

Chicken Kabobs

4 boneless skinless chicken breast halves
2 teaspoons ground mustard
1 tablespoon Worcestershire sauce
1/2 cup soy sauce
1/2 cup water
1 tablespoon vegetable oil
2 medium zucchini, cut in 1 1/2-inch slices
1 medium onion, cut in wedges
1 medium green pepper, cut into chunks
12 fresh mushrooms

Combine Worcestershire sauce and mustard. Add the soy sauce, water, and oil. Set aside 1/3 cup of the mixture for basting. Cut chicken into 1 1/2-inch pieces. Using a large resealable plastic bag, add the chicken and sauce to the bag. Refrigerate for a few hours, turning occasionally. Drain and discard the marinade.

Thread the vegetables and chicken on skewers. Baste with reserved sauce. Grill for 10 minutes. Rotate skewers, baste and cook for 10 minutes more or until chicken is done. Yield: 4 servings.

Best Barbecue Sauce for Chicken

1/2 cup butter or margarine
1/4 cup lemon juice
2 tablespoons ketchup
2 tablespoons vinegar
2 tablespoons horseradish
4 1/2 teaspoons Worcestershire sauce
2 teaspoons salt
3/4 teaspoon hot pepper sauce

Melt butter or margarine in a saucepan. Add remaining ingredients and simmer for 5 minutes. Baste chicken frequently as it grills over hot coals to get fully tangy flavor. Yield: 1 1/4 cups.

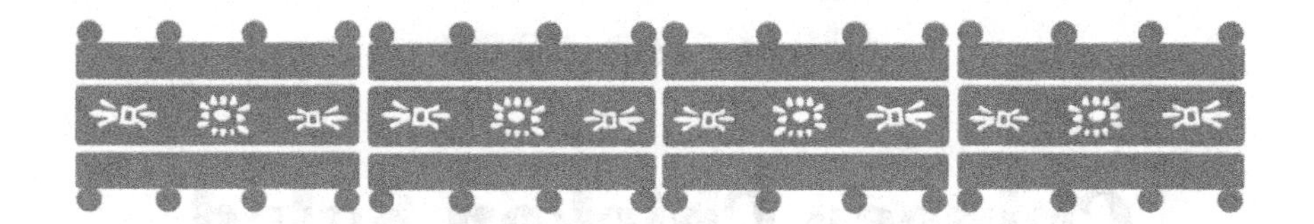

Chicken Salads

Chicken Salads

Chinese Chicken Salad

Marinate 2 boneless, skinless chicken breast halves overnight in:

1/4 cup soy sauce
1 clove garlic
4 teaspoons sugar

Drain and discard marinade. Bake at 350 degrees for 1 hour. Cool; shred chicken.

Add to:

1 head cabbage, sliced
4 green onions, sliced
4 tablespoons toasted sesame seeds
4 tablespoons toasted, sliced almonds
2 packages Top Ramen noodles (uncooked)

Dressing:

4 tablespoons sugar
1/2 cup sesame seed oil
1 teaspoon pepper
6 tablespoons rice vinegar
1/2 cup salad oil

Pour dressing on just before serving. Yield: 2 to 4 servings.

Pecan Chicken Salad with Grapes

4 boneless, skinless chicken breast halves, cooked and chopped
1/2 teaspoon curry powder
1 tablespoon vegetable oil
2 teaspoons minced candied gingerroot
2 tablespoons wine vinegar
2 tablespoons soy sauce
2 tablespoons onion, finely chopped
1 1/4 cups mayonnaise
1/2 cup water chestnuts, sliced
1/2 cup seedless green grapes
1/2 cup pecans, chopped
1/2 cup finely celery, chopped
Lettuce leaves
Sliced pineapple
Sliced avocado
Sliced hardboiled eggs
Paprika to taste

Heat curry powder in vegetable oil in a small skillet over medium heat until hot. Whisk the oil mixture together with gingerroot, wine vinegar, soy sauce, onion and mayonnaise in a large bowl. Add the chicken, water chestnuts, grapes, pecans and celery. Refrigerate, covered, until chilled. Serve over lettuce leaves with pineapple, avocado and eggs. Sprinkle with paprika. Yield: 18 servings.

Chicken Salad

2 cups cooked chicken, cubed
5 oz. (2 cups) rotini (corkscrew-shaped pasta)
1 cup mayo
1 1/2 teaspoons dry mustard
1/2 teaspoon paprika
1/4 teaspoon salt
1/4 teaspoon pepper
1 (20 oz.) can pineapple chunks, drained (save 3 tablespoons pineapple juice)
1 cup melon balls or cubes
1 cup green or red grapes, cut in half

Cook rotini; drain. Rinse in cold water. Combine the mayo, dry mustard, paprika, salt, pepper and the 3 tablespoons of drained pineapple juice. Mix. Add the chicken, melon, grapes and pineapple to the mayo mixture. Mix. Refrigerate before serving. Yield: 4 servings.

Tomatoes Stuffed with Chicken

1 cup diced, cooked chicken
8 medium size tomatoes
1/2 cup raw, sliced mushrooms
Lemon juice to taste
Salt and black pepper, to taste
1/4 cup mayonnaise
1/4 green bell pepper
Lettuce or parsley

To prepare tomatoes, cut a slice from the stem ends of tomatoes and scoop out the centers; sprinkle the tomato shells with salt and pepper and let stand 1/2 hour. Then invert on a plate to drain.

Combine mushrooms, chicken, lemon juice and mayonnaise. Spoon into tomatoes, rounding the tops slightly. Cut green pepper into short strips and arrange over tops. Serve on lettuce or parsley. Yield: 4 to 8 servings.

Cobb Salad

2 cups cooked chicken, diced
1 head lettuce (Boston, leaf, or chicory)
1/2 bunch water cress
2 large tomatoes, peeled and diced
2 avocados, peeled and diced
4 slices bacon, cooked
2 tablespoons scallions, chopped
4 oz. Roquefort cheese
2 hardboiled eggs, minced or grated
Minced parsley or chives (garnish)
1/2 cup French dressing

Wash lettuce, dry thoroughly and shred. Cut up the water cress. Line a flat salad bowl with greens. Put the chicken, tomatoes and avocados in three separate strips across the bowl.

Crumble crisp bacon over the salad. Add the scallions, grated or crumbled Roquefort cheese, and eggs; top with minced parsley or chives. Add the dressing and toss at table. Yield: 6 servings.

Chicken and Fruit Salad

3 cups cooked chicken, diced
1 cup celery, sliced
2 tablespoons green onion, chopped
2 tablespoons capers
1 teaspoon salt
2 tablespoons lemon juice
1 (11 oz.) can mandarin oranges, drained
1 (9 oz.) can pineapple tidbits, drained
1/2 cup slivered almonds
1/2 cup mayonnaise
1/2 teaspoon lemon peel

Combine chicken, celery, onions and capers. Mix salt and lemon juice and pour over chicken mixture. Chill for several hours. Just before serving, add fruit and nuts. Combine mayonnaise and lemon peel. Mix in carefully as not to break fruit. Yield: 6 servings.

Fajita Chicken Salad

2 boneless, skinless chicken breast halves
1/4 cup onion, chopped
1 package fajita marinade
Tortilla chips
4 to 5 cups shredded lettuce
1 1/2 cups shredded Colby or Monterey Jack cheese
1 medium tomato, chopped
Sour cream
Picante sauce
Guacamole

Cut chicken into bite-sized pieces. Place chicken and onion in shallow dish. Prepare fajita marinade according to package directions. Pour 1/2 the marinade over chicken. Let marinate in refrigerator for 15 minutes. Refrigerate remaining marinade for later use.

Arrange chips on 2 large plates. Top with lettuce, cheese and tomato. Drain and discard marinade from the chicken. Sauté chicken and onion in hot skillet with remaining marinade. Arrange chicken over salad. Serve with sour cream, picante sauce and guacamole. Yield: 2 servings.

Macadamia Nuts and Chicken Salad

4 boneless, skinless chicken breast halves, poached, and cut into 1 1/2-inch pieces
1 tart green apple, peeled and cut into 1-inch pieces
1 cup fresh pineapple, diced
1/2 cup white raisins or 1 cup seedless green grapes, halved
3 tablespoons chutney, chopped
1 cup mayonnaise
1 1/2 teaspoons curry powder
Salt to taste
1 cup coarsely chopped macadamia nuts
3 ripe cantaloupes, halved, seeded and peeled

In a bowl, combine the chicken, apple, pineapple, raisins or grapes, chutney, mayonnaise, curry powder, salt and nuts. Cover and refrigerate at least 3 before serving. Serve with chilled cantaloupes. Yield: 6 servings.

Asparagus-Chicken Salad

1 1/2 cups chopped, cooked chicken
1 lb. fresh asparagus
3 cups iceberg lettuce, torn
1/4 cup slivered almonds, toasted
1/4 cup fresh parsley, chopped
3 tablespoons raisins
1 medium-size apple, unpeeled and cut into 1/2 inch pieces
Creamy Blue Cheese Dressing

Snap off tough ends of asparagus. Remove scales with a knife or vegetable peeler. Place asparagus in a vegetable steamer over boiling water; cover and steam for 4 to 6 minutes or until tender crisp. Plunge asparagus into cold water; drain. Cut asparagus into 3/4-inch pieces.

Combine chicken, asparagus, torn lettuce, almonds, parsley, raisins, and apple; toss gently. Place mixture in a bowl and serve with Blue Cheese Dressing. Yield: 4 servings.

Pineapple Chicken Salad

4 cups cooked chicken, cubed
1 fresh pineapple
16 oz. package frozen bing cherries, thawed, drained
1/2 cup celery, sliced diagonally
1/4 cup green onions, chopped
1/2 teaspoon salt
1/8 teaspoon pepper
1/2 cup mayonnaise or salad dressing
1/2 cup dairy sour cream
1 tablespoon lemon juice
1 tablespoon finely chopped onion
Paprika

Cut pineapple lengthwise into 6 sections leaving green leaves intact. Cut out fleshy portion of each section; cut into 3/4-inch pieces. Set aside.

In a large bowl, combine chicken, cherries, celery, onions, salt and pepper. In a small bowl, combine mayonnaise or salad dressing, sour cream, lemon juice and onion; mix well. Add sauce to chicken mixture; toss until well coated. Cover and refrigerate for at least one hour.

Spoon salad mixture onto hollowed out pineapple sections and sprinkle salad lightly with paprika. Garnish with reserved pineapple pieces. Yield: 6 servings.

Cranberry-Pecan Chicken Salad

6 cups cooked chicken, chopped
4 green onions, thinly chopped
3 celery ribs, diced
1 (6 oz.) package sweetened dried cranberries
1/2 cup chopped pecans, toasted
1/2 cup honey mustard
3/4 cup mayonnaise
Garnish: lettuce leaves

Stir together chicken, onions, celery, cranberries, pecans, honey mustard and mayonnaise in a large bowl. Cover and refrigerate at least 1 hour or until ready to serve. Serve on lettuce leaves. Yield: 6 servings.

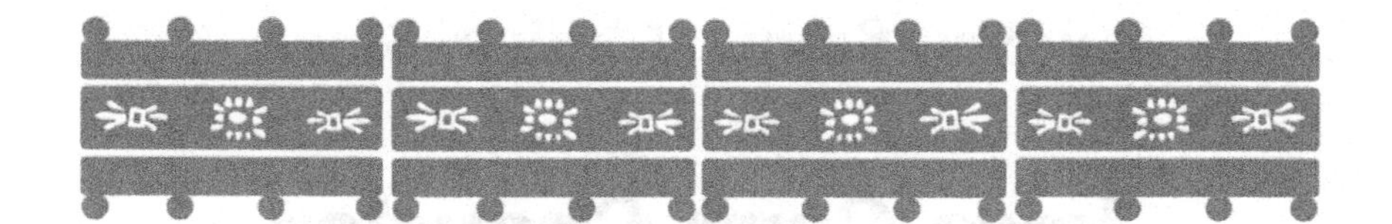

Chicken Soups, Chilies, Stews

Chicken Soups, Chilies, Stews

Iowa Corn Chowder

4 boneless, skinless chicken breast halves, cut into 1/2" cubes
3 slices bacon, diced
3/4 cup onion, finely chopped
3/4 cup celery, finely chopped
4 cups chicken broth
4 cups whole kernel corn
2 cups potatoes, diced
1/2 teaspoon salt
1 cup heavy or whipping cream
1/8 teaspoon pepper
2 tablespoons parsley, chopped

In a Dutch oven over medium heat, cook bacon until crisp. Remove bacon with slotted spoon and pour off all but 2 tablespoons of drippings. Add chicken, onion and celery to drippings in Dutch oven and cook, stirring frequently, 10 to 15 minutes or until tender.

In a blender, mix together 1 cup chicken broth and 2 cups corn. Mix on high speed until smooth. Add the pureed corn mixture to the chicken mixture in Dutch oven.

Add the remaining corn, potatoes, remaining chicken broth and salt. Bring to a boil over high heat, reduce to low and simmer partially covered for 20 minutes. Stir in cream, pepper and parsley. Simmer 2 to 3 minutes. Yield: 4 servings.

White Chili

8 boneless, skinless chicken breast halves
1 tablespoon vegetable oil
2 garlic cloves, minced
2 medium onions, chopped
4 (15 oz.) cans cannellini beans, rinsed & drained
2 (4 oz.) cans chopped green chilies
3 (14.5 oz.) cans chicken broth
1 teaspoon ground cumin
1 teaspoon salt
3/4 teaspoon oregano
1/2 teaspoon black pepper
1/2 teaspoon chili powder
1/8 teaspoon red pepper
1/8 teaspoon ground cloves
Sour cream

Cut chicken into 1 inch pieces. Heat oil in a Dutch oven over medium heat. Stir in chicken, garlic and onion to pan and cook for 10 minutes, or until chicken is thoroughly cooked and no longer pink in the center.

Stir in beans, chilies, broth, cumin, salt, oregano, black pepper, chili powder, cloves and red pepper; bring to boil. Reduce heat. Cover and simmer for 30 minutes. Top servings with sour cream. Yield: 10 cups.

Chicken Tomato Soup

1 deboned chicken, cooked and cut into pieces
2 teaspoons butter
1 large onion, chopped
1 small (4 oz.) package cream cheese
2 cans (15 oz. each) tomato sauce
4 cups milk
2 cloves garlic, chopped
3 cubes chicken bouillon
3 tomatoes, chopped
1 teaspoon hot sauce
1 teaspoon anise
2 zucchini, chopped

In a large saucepan or Dutch oven, melt butter and sauté chopped onion until onion is tender. Stir in cream cheese. Add tomato sauce, milk, garlic, chicken bouillon, chicken, tomatoes, hot sauce, anise and zucchini. Cook on medium heat until hot. Reduce heat to low, cover and simmer 45 minutes to one hour, stirring frequently.

Wild Rice Soup - Minnesota Style

2 cups cooked cubed chicken
6 tablespoons butter or margarine
1 tablespoon onions, minced
1/2 cup flour
2 1/2 cups chicken broth
1/2 cup carrots, finely shredded
2 cups cooked wild rice
1 cup half & half
2 tablespoons dry sherry
Parsley or chopped chives

Melt butter or margarine in a saucepan; sauté onions until tender. Add flour; gradually stir in chicken broth. Cook over medium heat, stirring constantly, until mixture comes to a boil. Boil and stir about 1 minute.

Add carrots, wild rice and chicken; simmer for 5 to 10 minutes. Add half & half and sherry. Simmer for 10 minutes or until hot. Garnish with parsley or chopped chives. Yield: 6 cups.

Chicken Tortellini Soup

2 cups diced, cooked chicken
6 1/2 cups water
1 (10.5 oz.) can cream of chicken soup
3 (10.5 oz.) cans condensed chicken broth
1 cup onions, chopped
1 cup carrots, sliced
2 garlic cloves, minced
1/2 teaspoon oregano
1/2 teaspoon basil
1 (16 oz.) package cheese tortellini
1 (10 oz.) package frozen chopped broccoli, thawed
Grated Parmesan cheese

In a large Dutch oven, mix together water, soup, chicken broth, chicken, onions, carrots, garlic, oregano and basil. Bring to a boil; add the tortellini. Simmer uncovered for 30 minutes. Add broccoli and simmer an additional 5 to10 minutes or until broccoli is tender. Sprinkle with Parmesan cheese. Yield: 8 to 10 servings.

Cream of Chicken Florentine

1 cup diced, cooked chicken
4 oz. butter or margarine
4 oz. flour
1 1/2 cups hot water
1/4 cup chicken broth
1 jar (4 oz.) diced pimento, drained
5 oz. frozen chopped spinach
1/2 teaspoon ground nutmeg
1 cup half and half
Seasoned croutons

In a Dutch oven over medium heat, melt butter or margarine. Add flour and stir until well blended and bubbly, about 2 to 3 minutes. Remove from heat. Stir in hot water, broth, pimento, spinach, nutmeg and half and half and heat to boiling. Reduce heat to medium-high and cook for 5 minutes, stirring occasionally. Serve hot garnished with croutons. Yield: 2 servings.

Tortilla Chip Soup

1 lb. boneless, skinless chicken breast, diced into 3/4" cubes
2 tablespoons vegetable oil
2 lb. tomatoes, diced or 1 (28 oz.) can diced tomatoes
1/2 green bell pepper, seeded and diced
2 (4 oz.) cans diced green chilies
1/2 large onion, diced
1/2 bunch cilantro, chopped
2 (14.5 oz.) cans chicken broth
2 tablespoons lime juice
1/2 teaspoon ground cumin
1/2 teaspoon black pepper
2 cups tortilla chips, crushed
1 cup Monterey Jack cheese, shredded

In a Dutch oven, brown the chicken in oil for about 8 minutes, 4 minutes on each side. Pour out excess oil and add all ingredients except chips and cheese. Simmer 20 minutes. Divide the crushed tortilla chips between 6 bowls and sprinkle with some cheese. Ladle the soup in the bowls and garnish with additional cheese. Yield: 6 servings.

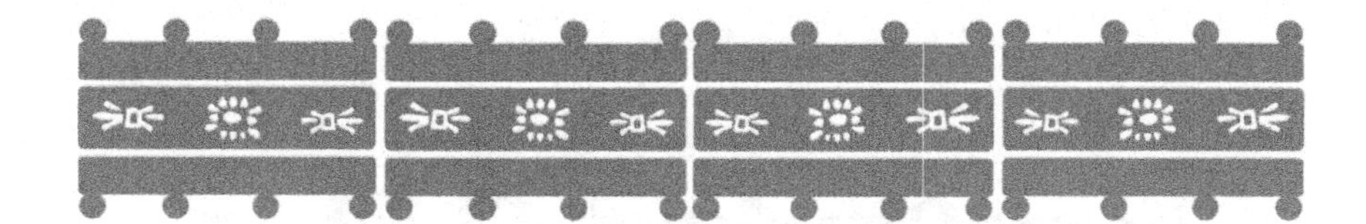

Slow Cooker Chicken

Slow Cooker Chicken

Easy Crockpot Chicken Enchiladas

4 boneless, skinless chicken breast halves
1 (4 oz.) can chopped green chilies
2 (10.5 oz.) cans cream of mushroom soup
8 to 10 corn tortillas
1 cup Cheddar cheese, shredded
Sour cream
Salsa
Olives

Combine chicken breasts, chilies and soup in a crockpot. Cook on low for 4 1/2 hours, stirring each hour.

Preheat oven to 350 degrees. Remove chicken breasts from crockpot and cut into bite-size pieces. Place chicken on tortillas, dividing equally. Roll up tortillas and place in baking dish. Spoon mushroom sauce from crockpot over tortillas to cover. Top with cheese. Bake for 15 to 20 minutes. Garnish with sour cream, salsa and olives. Yield: 8 servings.

Honey Barbecue Chicken

8 chicken drumsticks, skin removed
1/4 cup barbecue sauce
2 tablespoons honey
1/2 teaspoon dry mustard
1 (8 oz.) can pineapple tidbits in unsweetened juice, undrained
3 cups sweet potatoes, peeled and sliced
1/2 cup chicken broth
1/4 cup onion, finely chopped

In a bowl, combine barbecue sauce, honey and dry mustard. In a crockpot, mix together pineapple with liquid, sweet potatoes, chicken broth and onion. Dip chicken in barbecue sauce mixture, covering chicken well. Add chicken in a single layer over mixture in crockpot, overlapping if needed. Pour any remaining sauce mixture over chicken. Cover crockpot; cook on low for 7 to 10 hours or until sweet potatoes and chicken are tender. Yield: 4 servings.

Crockpot Chicken Stew

1 lb. chicken breasts, skinless, boneless
3 cups carrots
1/2 cup chicken broth
1 tablespoon brown sugar, packed
1/2 teaspoon hot sauce
2 tablespoons soy sauce
1/2 teaspoon ground ginger
1/2 teaspoon ground allspice
1 tablespoon cornstarch
1 (8 oz.) can pineapple chunks (reserve juice)
1 red bell pepper, diced

Cut the chicken and carrots into 1" pieces. Mix chicken, carrots, broth, brown sugar, hot sauce, soy sauce, ginger and allspice in a crockpot. Cook, covered, on low for 7 to 8 hours or until chicken is cooked through.

Blend cornstarch and reserved pineapple juice together and add to chicken mixture. Add bell pepper and pineapple and stir well. Cover and cook on high about 15 minutes or until slightly thickened and bubbly.

Crockpot Cacciatore

2 1/2 lbs. chicken thighs and drumsticks, skin removed
1 (8 oz.) package fresh mushrooms, sliced
Green bell pepper, cut into 1-inch pieces
1 (28 oz.) can crushed tomatoes, with juice
1 (1 oz.) envelope onion soup mix
1/2 teaspoon dried basil
1/4 cup dry red wine

Place mushrooms and bell pepper in crockpot and add the chicken pieces on top. In a bowl, combine tomatoes, soup mix, basil and wine. Pour tomato mixture over chicken in crockpot. Cover. Cook on high 4 to 6 hours or low 8 to 10 hours. Yield: 4 servings.

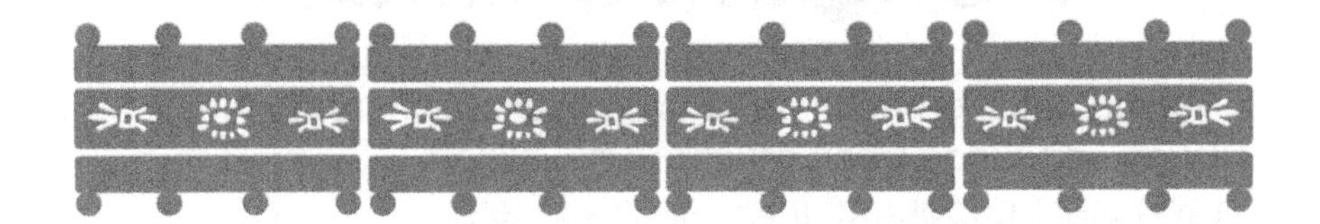

Skillet Chicken

Skillet Chicken

Chicken Parmesan

4 boneless, skinless chicken breast halves
1 egg, slightly beaten
1/2 cup seasoned dry bread crumbs
2 tablespoons butter
2 cups spaghetti sauce
1/2 cup shredded Mozzarella cheese
1 teaspoon dried parsley flakes
1 tablespoon grated Parmesan cheese
4 cups hot cooked spaghetti

Flatten chicken to an even thickness using meat mallet or rolling pin. Dip chicken in egg; coat with crumbs. In a large skillet over medium heat, melt butter; add chicken and cook until browned on both sides for about 8 minutes, 4 minutes on each side.

Reduce heat to low and add spaghetti sauce. Cover and cook for 10 minutes. Sprinkle with Mozzarella cheese, parsley Parmesan cheese and. Cover and cook for 5 minutes, or until cheese melts. Serve over hot spaghetti. Yield: 4 servings.

Cashew Chicken Stir-Fry

4 to 6 boneless, skinless chicken breasts
2 tablespoons cornstarch
2 tablespoons chicken broth
2 tablespoons soy sauce
1 tablespoon vegetable oil
1 red bell pepper
1 green bell pepper
1/2 cup onions, sliced
1 cup mushrooms, chopped
1/2 small clove garlic (minced)
1 can water chestnuts (drain & reserve 1/4 cup liquid)
3 oz. cashews
2 tablespoons Hoisin sauce
Hot cooked rice

Cut chicken into chunks. Put chicken in a bowl, sprinkle with cornstarch and toss to coat. Add chicken broth and soy sauce. Marinate for 15 minutes. Stir fry chicken in skillet or wok in oil until cooked through and chicken is no longer pink in the center.

Microwave peppers and onions on MEDIUM for 2 minutes. Add to chicken, then add mushrooms, garlic, water chestnuts, cashews and Hoisin sauce. Cook until heated through, about 10 to 15 minutes. Serve with rice. Yield: 4 servings.

Easy Chinese Chicken with Vegetables

2 boneless, skinless chicken breast halves
3 tablespoons peanut oil or olive oil
1 clove garlic, minced
1 large onion, peeled and sliced
2 medium carrots, peeled and sliced
1 (7 oz.) package frozen pea pods
1/4 lb. fresh mushrooms, sliced
1 (8 oz.) can water chestnuts, drained and sliced
2 chicken bouillon cubes
1 cup hot water
1 1/2 tablespoons cornstarch
2 tablespoons soy sauce
Hot cooked rice

Cut chicken into bite-size pieces. Heat oil in a wok or large skillet. Quickly sauté the chicken, garlic and onion for about 2 minutes. Add carrots; stir fry 5 minutes. Add pea pods, mushrooms, and water chestnuts and stir fry for 2 to 3 minutes on medium-high heat or until chicken is no longer pink in the center.

Dissolve bouillon cubes in hot water; add to chicken and vegetables. Mix cornstarch and soy sauce; stir into chicken mixture. Bring to a boil. Serve over rice. Yield: 6 servings.

Coconut-Cherry Chicken

4 boneless, skinless chicken breast halves
1 tablespoon cornstarch
2 tablespoons lemon juice
2 1/2 cups fresh or canned dark sweet cherries, pitted
1/3 cup flour
1/2 teaspoon cinnamon
1/2 teaspoon allspice
1/2 cup water
1/4 cup toasted, shredded coconut

Stir together cornstarch and lemon juice; stir in cherries and set aside. Combine flour, cinnamon and allspice in a bag; add chicken and shake to coat. Brown chicken in skillet sprayed with non-stick cooking spray over medium-high heat for about 8 minutes, 4 minutes on each side. Add 1/2 cup water. Reduce heat; cover and simmer about 20 minutes, or until chicken is no longer pink inside.

Remove chicken from skillet and cover with foil. Drain all except 1 tablespoon of drippings from pan; place cherry mixture in pan and bring to a boil. Cook until mixture thickens. Pour cherry mixture over chicken and garnish with coconut. Yield: 4 servings.

Chinese Chicken

4 boneless, skinless chicken breast halves
3 tablespoons olive oil
1 green pepper, cut in strips
1 medium onion, cut in pieces
1 cup celery, sliced
1 (5 oz.) can sliced water chestnuts
1 cup chicken broth
1 teaspoon salt
1/8 teaspoon pepper
2 tablespoons soy sauce
2 teaspoons cornstarch

Cut chicken breasts into thin strips. Heat oil in skillet. Add chicken and cook, stirring occasionally, about 3 minutes. Add green pepper, onion, celery, water chestnuts, broth and salt and pepper. Cover and cook 5 minutes or until chicken is no longer pink inside. Combine soy sauce and cornstarch and add to skillet. Stir until thickened. Serve on rice or chow mein noodles. Yield: 4 servings.

Coq Au Vin

2 (2-lb.) whole chickens, cut into pieces
1/4 cup flour
1 tablespoon Season All
1/2 teaspoon paprika
1/4 teaspoon black pepper
1/8 teaspoon nutmeg
1/2 cup butter
1/4 cup cognac or other brandy
1 cup dry red wine
12 small white onions
12 small whole mushrooms or 1 (8 oz.) can mushrooms
1/2 teaspoon rosemary
1/4 teaspoon thyme
1/8 teaspoon garlic powder
1 teaspoon parsley

Cut chicken in pieces. In a large resealable plastic bag, combine flour, Season All, paprika, pepper and nutmeg. Add chicken and shake to coat with flour mixture. Melt butter in large skillet and add chicken. Cook on medium heat until chicken is browned, about 8 minutes.

Remove pan from heat, pour cognac over chicken. Put pan back on heat and light with a long match held just above the pot (lighting the fumes). When the flames die out (within one minute), add wine, onions, mushrooms, rosemary, thyme, garlic powder and parsley. Simmer, covered, for 1 hour or until chicken is tender. Yield: 4 servings.

Chicken Piccata

2 boneless, skinless chicken breast halves
1/4 cup flour
6 tablespoons butter
1/2 cup vermouth or dry wine
1/4 cup chicken stock
1/4 cup chopped fresh parsley
Salt and pepper to taste
Noodles or rice
Capers

Cut chicken into 2 inch pieces. Dredge in flour. Melt butter in skillet over medium heat. Add chicken and cook until lightly browned, about 4 minutes per side. Add Vermouth or wine, broth and parsley. Season with salt and pepper. Reduce heat to low. Cover and cook until chicken is opaque, 8 to 10 minutes. Serve over noodles or rice; garnish with capers. Yield: 2 servings.

Chicken, Nicoise Style

5 lbs. chicken pieces
Salt and pepper to taste
3 tablespoons olive oil
2 tablespoons butter
1 large onion, diced
3 cloves garlic, minced
1/2 cup mushrooms, sliced
2 bay leaves
1/4 teaspoon thyme
1/4 teaspoon leaf tarragon
4 large tomatoes, peeled and quartered
1 cup dry white wine
1 cup chicken broth, canned
12 pitted green olives, sliced
12 pitted ripe olives, sliced

Salt and pepper chicken. Brown in oil and butter on both sides, about 8 minutes. Remove chicken and sauté onion, garlic, and mushrooms for several minutes until soft. Replace chicken and turn down heat to simmer. Add bay leaves, thyme, tarragon, tomatoes, wine and broth. Cover and cook for 1 hour. Add olives and cook for 10 minutes longer. Yield: 6 servings.

Italian Chicken Breasts

4 bone-in chicken breast halves
1/4 teaspoon pepper
2 tablespoons olive or vegetable oil
1 medium onion, chopped
1/2 cup dry white wine
1 (16 oz.) can tomatoes, undrained
1 clove minced garlic
1 tablespoon fresh parsley, chopped
1/2 teaspoon pepper
1 teaspoon dried sweet basil
1 teaspoon dried oregano
4 fresh mushrooms, sliced

Remove the skin and fat from the chicken breasts. Season the breasts with pepper, and sauté in oil about 10 minutes. Add onion, wine, tomatoes, garlic, parsley, pepper, basil and oregano. Cover and cook for 30 minutes. Add mushrooms to the pan and cook for an additional 5 minutes until the mushrooms are tender. Yield: 4 servings.

Chicken Fried Rice

1 cup finely chopped, cooked chicken
4 cups cold cooked rice (must be cold, best if refrigerated overnight)
3 tablespoons peanut or sesame oil
6 green onions (chopped including greens)
1 cup frozen peas
2 tablespoons soy sauce
Salt and pepper to taste
2 or 3 eggs

Sauté rice in hot peanut or sesame oil in wok on medium heat for 15 minutes or until golden brown. Add onions, peas, soy sauce and salt and pepper, stir 5 minutes. Make 3-inch well in center, add a drop of oil, crack eggs into well and scramble with spatula. When egg is cooked, mix into rice mixture. Add chicken and toss until heated through. Yield: 6 servings.

Chicken and Peppers

2 boneless, skinless chicken breast halves, cut into 1" squares
1 envelope Lipton onion soup mix
3 tablespoons soy sauce
3 tablespoons vegetable oil
1 clove garlic, minced
3 teaspoons cornstarch
3 ribs celery, cut into 1/2" pieces
1 green bell pepper, cut into 1" pieces
1 red pepper, cut into 1" pieces
8 green onions, cut into 1/2" slices (including green tops)
1/2 teaspoon sugar
3/4 cup cold water

In a bowl, mix together chicken, onion soup mix, 1 tablespoon soy sauce, 1 tablespoon oil, garlic, and 1 teaspoon corn starch; marinate in refrigerator for 20 minutes.

In a large skillet, heat remaining oil; cook celery, green pepper and red pepper over high heat, stirring frequently for 3 minutes; add green onions and cook 2 minutes; remove from pan. Add chicken to skillet and cook 3 minutes or until chicken is no longer pink in the center. In a bowl, combine remaining 2 tablespoons soy sauce and 2 teaspoons cornstarch with sugar and water. Add soy sauce mixture to skillet with vegetables; simmer 3 minutes. Yield: 4 servings.

Honolulu Chicken

6 boneless, skinless chicken breasts
1/4 cup flour
1/8 teaspoon salt
1/8 teaspoon pepper
2 tablespoons vegetable oil
1 (10 oz.) jar peach preserves
1/2 cup barbecue sauce
1/2 cup onion, chopped
2 tablespoons soy sauce
1 green pepper, cut into strips
1 (8 oz.) can of water chestnuts
Hot cooked rice

Combine flour, salt and pepper in a large resealable plastic bag. Add chicken to bag and shake to coat chicken. In a skillet, cook chicken in hot oil for about 10 minutes, until browned, and drain. Combine preserves, barbecue sauce, onion and soy sauce; pour over chicken. Cover and simmer for 1 hour. Add green pepper and water chestnuts. Serve with rice. Yield: 6 servings.

Lemon Chicken Stir Fry

1 lb. boneless, skinless chicken breasts, cut into strips
1/2 cup water
1/4 cup lemon juice
1 tablespoon cornstarch
1 chicken bouillon cube
2 teaspoons soy sauce
2 teaspoons apple juice
1 teaspoon chili sauce
2 tablespoons vegetable oil
2 garlic cloves, crushed
4 cups cut up fresh vegetables (onion, mushroom, carrot, red pepper, broccoli, celery, snow peas, etc.)
Hot cooked rice

Combine water, lemon juice, cornstarch, bouillon cube, soy sauce, apple juice and chili sauce in a small bowl until well mixed; set aside.

Heat oil in wok or skillet over medium heat. Cook garlic and chicken until chicken is no longer pink inside, about 10 minutes, stirring often. Add vegetables. Cook and stir about 5 minutes or until heated through; add lemon juice mixture until sauce is thickened and bubbling. Serve over rice. Yield: 4 servings.

Linguine Abbasini

1 lb. boneless, skinless chicken breast, cut into strips
3/4 lb. linguine
3 tablespoons olive oil
3 teaspoons garlic, minced
1/4 cup flour
4 tablespoons white wine
3 tablespoons scallions, chopped
1 oz. sun-dried tomatoes in oil, chopped
8 large fresh mushrooms
1/8 teaspoon white pepper
2 cups chicken broth
1 tablespoon fresh basil, chopped

Cook linguine in boiling water (add 1 teaspoon salt and 1 tablespoon olive oil) until al dente (firm to the bite). Drain.

Heat 3 tablespoons olive oil and garlic in a skillet for 1 minute. Coat chicken in flour and add to oil. Sauté just until chicken is no longer pink in center. Add wine, scallions, tomatoes, mushrooms, pepper, and chicken broth and simmer 5 minutes. Add pasta; toss. Top with basil and serve. Yield: 4 servings.

Chicken Diane

8 boneless, skinless chicken breast halves
1/4 cup flour
1/4 cup butter or margarine
1 small tomato, chopped
3 tablespoons lemon juice
3 tablespoons Worcestershire sauce
2 tablespoons onions, chopped
2 tablespoons green pepper, chopped
1/2 teaspoon salt
2 teaspoons ketchup
1 teaspoon prepared mustard

In a shallow dish, place flour and add chicken, one piece at a time, dredging to coat. Melt butter in a skillet over medium heat; add chicken and cook, turning, about 25 minutes or until light golden brown and fork can be inserted in each piece with ease. Remove chicken to serving platter and keep warm.

Pour fat off juices in skillet and add to skillet tomato, lemon juice, Worcestershire, onion, green pepper, salt, ketchup and mustard. Stir to mix. Simmer, uncovered, for about 2 minutes. To serve, pour mixture over hot chicken. Yield: 4 servings.

Le Coq De Chicken

8 boneless, skinless chicken breast halves
2 tablespoons vegetable oil
2 tablespoons olive oil
Salt and pepper to taste
2 tablespoons flour
2 tablespoons tomato paste
1 clove garlic, pressed
1 cup dry white wine
1 (14.5 oz.) can chicken broth
1 bay leaf
1 teaspoon thyme
2 tablespoons butter
1/2 lb. fresh mushrooms, sliced
1 large onion, chopped

Heat vegetable and olive oil together in skillet and brown chicken well on both sides for about 4 minutes on each side. Sprinkle with flour, salt and pepper; add tomato paste, garlic, wine, chicken broth, bay leaf, and thyme. Simmer about 10 minutes.

In a separate pan, sauté mushrooms and onions in butter. Add to chicken, simmer until chicken is just done, about 30 minutes. Remove bay leaf before serving. Yield: 4 servings.

Chicken and Broccoli Stir-Fry

2 boneless, skinless chicken breast halves
1 tablespoon cornstarch
1/4 cup corn syrup
2 tablespoons soy sauce
2 tablespoons dry sherry
Cayenne pepper to taste
5 tablespoons olive oil
1 tablespoon minced garlic
2 cups broccoli, chopped
3/4 cup mushrooms, sliced
1 (8 oz.) can water chestnuts, sliced
1/2 cup chicken broth
2 cups brown rice (prepared according to package)

Combine cornstarch, corn syrup, soy sauce, sherry and cayenne pepper; set aside. Cut chicken breasts into thin strips and stir-fry in olive oil with garlic. Add broccoli, mushrooms, and water chestnuts; continue stir-frying until chicken is no longer pink inside. Lower heat and add soy sauce mixture and chicken broth. After it thickens, serve with brown rice. Yield: 4 servings.

Tasty Low-Fat Chicken Fettuccini

4 boneless, skinless chicken breast halves
1 medium onion, diced
2 teaspoons minced garlic
2 tablespoons olive oil
26 oz. light spaghetti sauce
1 large tomato
1 green bell pepper, diced
1 tablespoon basil
12 oz. fettuccini pasta

Sauté onion and minced garlic in olive oil at low heat. Cut chicken breasts into small pieces and add to oil. Once chicken is slightly cooked, add spaghetti sauce, tomato, green pepper and basil. Cover and simmer until chicken is no longer pink in the center. Prepare pasta according to directions on package. Drain pasta and place in bowl. Add sauce mixture to pasta and serve with low-fat bread sticks. Yield: 4 servings.

Country Fried Chicken

1 (2 1/2 to 3-lb.) whole chicken, cut into pieces
1 cup flour
2 teaspoons garlic salt
1 teaspoon black pepper
1 teaspoon paprika
1/4 teaspoon poultry seasoning
1/2 cup milk
1 egg, beaten
Vegetable oil

Mix together flour, garlic salt, pepper, paprika and poultry seasoning. Dip chicken pieces in flour mixture. Combine milk and egg. Dip chicken pieces in milk mixture, then dip in flour mixture again.

In a large skillet, heat 1/4 inch of oil. Fry chicken on all sides until brown for about 8 minutes. Cover and simmer for about 40 to 45 minutes or until tender, turning occasionally. Remove cover and cook for 5 more minutes. Yield: 4 servings.

Chicken on Angel Hair Pasta

1 package (12 oz.) angel hair pasta
3 boneless, skinless chicken breast halves
1 tablespoon olive oil
2 cups baby carrots, cut in half lengthwise
2 cups broccoli florets
1/4 cup water
1 teaspoon chicken bouillon granules
1 jar (28 oz.) chunky-style pasta sauce
1/3 cup grated Parmesan cheese

Cook pasta according to package instructions; drain. While pasta is cooking, cut chicken into 1-inch cubes. Heat oil in large non-stick skillet over medium heat. Add chicken; cook and stir 5 minutes. Stir in carrots and broccoli, water and chicken bouillon. Reduce heat to low; cover and cook 5 minutes or until vegetables are crisply tender and chicken is no longer pink in the center.

Place pasta sauce in a saucepan and bring to a boil over high heat. Serve pasta topped with sauce and chicken and vegetable mixture. Sprinkle with cheese. Yield: 6 servings.

Creole Jambalaya

3 cups cooked chicken, chopped
1 lb. smoked pork sausage
1 cup green bell pepper, chopped
1 cup onion, chopped
1 clove of garlic, crushed
1 tablespoon flour
1 (28 oz.) can tomatoes
2 1/2 cups water
2 tablespoons fresh parsley, chopped
2 cups uncooked rice
2 tablespoons Worcestershire sauce
1/2 teaspoon thyme
2 teaspoons salt
1/4 teaspoon red pepper

Cut the sausage into 1/2-inch pieces. Brown sausage in a large skillet for 5 minutes. Drain, reserving 2 tablespoons of sausage drippings. Remove sausage; set aside.

Sauté the bell pepper, onion and garlic in the reserved drippings in the skillet. Stir in the flour. Cook over low heat until brown, stirring frequently. Stir in the tomatoes, water and parsley. Bring to a boil. Add the sausage, rice, Worcestershire sauce, thyme, salt and red pepper. Simmer, covered, for 20 minutes. Add the chicken. Simmer for 10 minutes longer; fluff with a fork. Yield: 12 servings.

Chicken with Apples

4 boneless, skinless chicken breast halves
1 tablespoon olive oil
1 cup apple juice
1 Granny Smith apple, peeled and sliced
1 garlic clove, minced
1 onion, thinly sliced
1/2 teaspoon salt
1/2 teaspoon thyme
2 tablespoons Dijon mustard

Pound the chicken to a 3/4-inch thickness with a meat mallet or rolling pin. Heat olive oil in a large skillet over medium-high heat. Add chicken and sauté until golden brown, about 4 minutes on each side. Stir in apple juice, apple, garlic, onion, salt and thyme and reduce heat. Simmer, covered, for 6 to 8 minutes or until the chicken is cooked through and no longer pink in the center.

Remove the chicken, apple and onion with a slotted spoon to a platter and keep warm. Bring the pan juices to a boil and cook to reduce the liquid, stirring constantly. Whisk in the Dijon mustard and serve over the chicken, apple and onion. Yield: 4 servings.

Blackened Chicken

6 boneless, skinless chicken breast halves
1 tablespoon salt
1 tablespoon paprika
1 teaspoon black pepper
1/2 teaspoon onion powder
1/2 teaspoon garlic powder
1/2 teaspoon chili powder
1/2 teaspoon thyme
1/2 teaspoon oregano
1/2 teaspoon cayenne pepper
3 tablespoons butter or margarine, melted

Combine the salt, paprika, black pepper, onion powder, garlic powder, chili powder, thyme, oregano and cayenne pepper in a bowl. Pound the chicken to a 1/4-inch thickness with a meat mallet or rolling pin.

Heat a heavy skillet over medium-high heat until hot. Brush the chicken on both sides with melted butter or margarine and sprinkle with the paprika mixture. Place 3 chicken breasts in the hot skillet. When blackened on one side, turn to the other side; chicken will cook quickly. Chicken is done when it is no longer pink in the center. Yield: 6 servings.

General Tsao's Chicken

The chicken is stir-fried rather than deep-fried in this traditional dish. You'll love the great Asian flavor.

1 lb. boneless, skinless chicken breast halves
2 teaspoons peanut oil
2 scallions, chopped
2 garlic cloves, minced
1/2 teaspoon red pepper flakes
3/4 cup chicken broth
2 tablespoons soy sauce
2 tablespoons sugar
2 tablespoons cornstarch
1 tablespoon white wine vinegar
1/2 teaspoon ginger
2 cups cooked rice

Rinse the chicken and pat dry. Cut into 2-inch pieces. Heat the peanut oil in a large skillet over medium-high heat. Add the scallions, garlic and red pepper flakes. Stir-fry for 2 minutes. Add the chicken and stir-fry for 5 minutes or until browned.

Whisk the chicken broth, soy sauce, sugar, cornstarch, vinegar and ginger together in a bowl. Add to the skillet. Cook for 3 minutes or until the sauce thickens and the chicken is cooked through. Serve over rice. Yield: 4 servings.

Greek Cinnamon Chicken

1 tablespoon olive oil
4 garlic cloves, minced
2 onions, chopped
6 (4 oz.) boneless skinless chicken thighs
1/4 cup dry white wine
1 (15 oz.) can diced tomatoes (undrained)
1 cinnamon stick
2 bay leaves
1/2 teaspoon pepper
1/2 teaspoon ground cinnamon
1/4 teaspoon salt
6 cups hot cooked couscous

Over medium heat, heat olive oil in a large skillet. Sauté the garlic and onions in the hot oil for about 5 minutes or until tender. Add the chicken, wine, undrained tomatoes, cinnamon stick, bay leaves, pepper, ground cinnamon and salt; bring to a boil. Reduce the heat and simmer, covered, for about 30 minutes or until the chicken is cooked through. Remove and discard the bay leaves and cinnamon stick. Serve over couscous. Yield: 2 to 4 servings.

Breast of Chicken Juliet

8 bone-in chicken breast halves
1/4 cup margarine
1 (6 oz.) can sliced mushrooms, drained
2/3 cup light cream
2 (10.5 oz.) cans cream of chicken soup
1 large garlic clove, minced
1/8 teaspoon crushed thyme
1/8 teaspoon crushed rosemary

In a large skillet, brown chicken in margarine for about 8 minutes, 4 minutes on each side. Remove chicken from skillet. Add mushrooms to skillet and brown. Stir in soup, garlic, thyme and rosemary. Add chicken. Cook, covered, over low heat 45 minutes, stirring occasionally. Blend in cream, heat slowly to serving temperature. Yield: 8 servings.

Chicken Chow Mein

1 lb. boneless, skinless chicken breast halves
3 tablespoons corn oil
1 clove garlic, minced
6 mushrooms, sliced
2 stalks celery, diagonally sliced
1 (8 oz.) can bean sprouts, drained
1/4 cup canned sliced bamboo shoots (drained)
1 cup chicken bouillon
1 teaspoon salt
2 tablespoons cornstarch
1/2 cup water
1 teaspoon soy sauce
Chow Mein noodles

Cut chicken into thin strips. Heat corn oil in skillet. Add chicken and garlic; sauté 5 minutes, stirring occasionally. Add mushrooms, celery, bean sprouts, bamboo shoots, bouillon, and salt. Cook over medium heat 3 minutes.

Blend cornstarch, water and soy sauce. Stir into mixture in skillet. Cook, stirring constantly, until sauce is slightly thickened and transparent. Serve with Chow Mein noodles. Yield: 6 servings.

Southern Pacific Chicken

1 (2 1/2 to 3 1/2-lb.) chicken pieces, skinned and cut into 8 pieces
3 tablespoons flour
1/2 teaspoon black pepper
1 tablespoon olive oil
1 tablespoon butter or margarine
4 oz. fresh mushrooms, sliced
1 clove garlic, minced
1 large onion, finely chopped
1/2 cup dry white wine or low-sodium chicken broth
1/2 teaspoon salt
2 teaspoons butter or margarine
4 slices white bread, cut in 1/2-in. cubes
1/8 teaspoon garlic powder
2 tablespoons parsley, minced

On a plate, mix flour and pepper; coat chicken in flour mixture. In 12-inch non-stick skillet, heat oil over medium high heat. Add chicken; brown 4 minutes on each side. Transfer to a platter.

Melt butter or margarine in the same skillet. Add mushrooms, garlic and onion; sauté for 5 minutes or until vegetables are tender. Add chicken, wine or broth, and salt; bring to a boil. Lower heat; cover and simmer, stirring often, for 30 minutes or until juices run clear when thigh is pricked with fork. Transfer to warm platter; cover with foil.

Meanwhile, prepare croutons: In 10-inch non-stick skillet, heat butter and oil over moderately high heat. Add bread cubes and garlic powder; stir 4 minutes or until croutons are browned. Spoon on top of chicken; sprinkle with parsley. Yield: 4 servings.

Garden Chicken Skillet

1 (2 1/2 to 3 1/2-lb.) chicken pieces
1/4 cup vegetable oil
1/4 cup flour
Salt and pepper to taste
3/4 cup chicken broth
3/4 cup cooking sherry
1 (8 oz.) package frozen artichoke hearts
2 tomatoes, cut in wedges
1 onion, sliced
1/2 green pepper, sliced

Heat the oil in a skillet. Mix the flour with salt and pepper; dredge chicken in seasoned flour. Brown chicken slowly in oil, turning once, for about 8 minutes. Turn heat to low; add broth and sherry. Cover; cook for 45 minutes. Push the chicken to side; add artichoke hearts, tomatoes, onion, and green pepper; cook for about 15 minutes. Yield: 4 servings.

Saucy Chicken Breasts

6 to 8 boneless, skinless chicken breast halves
1 egg mixed with 1 tablespoon water
1 cup seasoned bread crumbs
1/8 teaspoon salt
1/8 teaspoon pepper
1/8 teaspoon paprika
3 tablespoons butter or margarine
1 cup red currant jelly
1 cup chili sauce
1 cup dry sherry

Preheat oven to 400 degrees F. Combine jelly, chili sauce and sherry in medium saucepan. Heat over low to medium heat, stirring occasionally until thickened, 30 to 45 minutes.

Meanwhile, flatten each chicken breast by pounding with a rolling pin or mallet. Dip each breast into egg mixture then into bread crumbs. Season with salt, pepper and paprika. Roll and secure with a toothpick. Season again. In a large skillet, sauté chicken in butter until lightly golden, turning gently with two forks or tongs to brown evenly. Remove chicken from heat. Place chicken in shallow pan or baking dish and remove the toothpicks. Cover with sauce and bake about 20 minutes or until done. Yield: 6 to 8 servings.

Cashew Chicken

4 boneless, skinless chicken breast halves
1 cup milk
1 cup flour
1 cup cornstarch
1 to 2 cups vegetable oil
1 (10.5 oz.) can chicken broth
3 tablespoons oyster sauce
1 tablespoon sugar
1 teaspoon pepper
2 tablespoons corn starch
1/4 cup water
4 cups cooked rice
3 green onions, chopped
1 cup cashews

Preheat oven to 200 degrees F. Cut chicken breasts into bite-sized pieces. Place in bowl. Add milk to cover. Soak for 15 minutes. Coat chicken with flour, then cornstarch. In a skillet over medium-high heat, heat oil until hot. Add chicken using a slotted spoon. Fry 10 to 15 minutes, turning occasionally, until chicken is golden brown and center is no longer pink. Remove chicken with slotted spoon and keep warm in oven.

Bring chicken broth to a boil in saucepan. Add oyster sauce, sugar and pepper. Remove from heat. Combine cornstarch with water in small bowl. Add to broth, stirring constantly with wire whisk until desired consistency. Serve chicken on rice. Pour sauce over top. Garnish with green onions and cashews. Yield: 4 servings.

Kung Pao Chicken

1 lb. boneless, skinless chicken breasts
1 tablespoon cornstarch
2 teaspoons peanut oil
2 cloves of garlic, minced
1 bunch green onions, cut in 1/2" pieces, including green tops
1/4 teaspoon ground ginger
1/4 teaspoon red pepper flakes
2 teaspoons sugar
2 tablespoons soy sauce
2 tablespoons wine vinegar
1/2 cup dry roasted peanuts
Rice

Cut chicken into 1-inch pieces. Combine with cornstarch in a bowl; toss to coat. In a wok or large skillet, heat oil on medium-high heat. Add chicken and cook, stirring constantly, for 6 to 8 minutes or until chicken is no longer pink in the center. Remove chicken from skillet.

Cut onions, including tops, into 1/2" pieces. Add garlic, onions, ginger and red pepper to the skillet. Stir fry for 1 minute, then remove from heat. Combine sugar, soy sauce and vinegar in a bowl. Add soy sauce mixture to skillet. Return chicken to skillet. Stir until chicken is well coated. Stir in peanuts. Cook for 10 minutes on medium heat until hot, stirring occasionally. Serve over rice. Yield: 2 to 4 servings.

Chicken with Mushrooms

2 boneless, skinless chicken breast halves
1 teaspoon cornstarch
1 tablespoon sherry
1 tablespoon vegetable oil
1/2 teaspoon salt
1/8 teaspoon ginger
3/4 cup broccoli florets, chopped
1/4 cup bamboo shoots
1/2 cup canned or fresh mushrooms, chopped
12 snow peas or more
5 water chestnuts, sliced
1/4 cup chicken broth or water
1 tablespoon vegetable oil

2 teaspoons cornstarch
2 teaspoons water
1/8 teaspoon pepper
1/4 teaspoon sugar

Slice chicken breast into thin strips; mix with 1 teaspoon cornstarch and sherry. Heat 1 tablespoon oil, add salt and ginger. Add broccoli, bamboo shoots, mushrooms, snow peas and water chestnuts, stir for 30 seconds. Add chicken broth or water, cover and cook for 2 minutes. Remove from heat and set aside.

Heat 1 tablespoon vegetable oil and cook the chicken about 5 minutes until it is lightly browned on the edges and is no longer pink in the middle. In a bowl, mix 2 teaspoons cornstarch, water, pepper and sugar and add to chicken mixture. Bring to a boil, stirring constantly, until the sauce thickens. Add the vegetable mixture to the chicken and toss to coat with sauce. Yield: 2 servings.

Chicken Veracruz

4 skinless, boneless chicken breast halves
1 teaspoon olive oil
Salt and pepper to taste
1 (14.5 oz.) can of Mexican-style stewed tomatoes
1/2 cup green olives with pimientos, chopped

12 oz. fresh herb-flavored linguine

In a large non-stick skillet, heat oil. Flatten the chicken breasts slightly with a rolling pin or mallet. Sprinkle with salt and pepper to taste. When the oil is hot, add the chicken and cook over high heat for 3 minutes. Turn the chicken over. Add the stewed tomatoes, breaking them up slightly with a spoon. Stir in the green olives. Reduce heat to medium and continue cooking until the chicken is tender and cooked through, about 3 minutes longer.

In a pot of salted boiling water, cook linguine until tender, but still firm, about 2 to 3 minutes. Drain pasta and pour onto serving platter. Arrange chicken breasts on top, spoon sauce over chicken and serve. Yield: 4 servings.

Chinese Chicken

4 boneless, skinless chicken breast halves, cut into thin bite-sized strips
1 (6 oz.) package uncooked rice noodles
2 teaspoons vegetable oil
1 (9 oz.) package frozen cut broccoli, thawed, drained
2 cups fresh bean sprouts
1 (8 oz.) can bamboo shoots, drained
1/2 cup water
2 tablespoons soy sauce
1 teaspoon sugar
4 teaspoons cornstarch
1/2 teaspoon chicken instant bouillon

Cook rice noodles as directed on package. Drain; cover to keep warm. Heat oil in a Dutch oven or large skillet over medium-high heat until hot. Add chicken; cook 5 or 6 minutes or until chicken is no longer pink in center. Add broccoli, bean sprouts and bamboo shoots; cook until vegetables are tender, about 5 minutes, stirring occasionally.

In a small bowl, mix together water, soy sauce, sugar, cornstarch and chicken bouillon. Add to skillet; cook and stir until thickened. Serve chicken over hot rice noodles. Yield: 4 servings.

Quick Saucy Chicken

8 boneless, skinless chicken breast halves
2 tablespoons butter or margarine
1 clove garlic, pressed
3 green onions, finely chopped
1 tablespoon flour
2 tablespoons fresh parsley, chopped
1/2 cup heavy cream
3/4 cup grated Swiss cheese
1/3 cup freshly grated Parmesan cheese
1/2 teaspoon salt
1/8 teaspoon black pepper
Hot cooked pasta or rice

Cut the chicken into very thin strips. Heat the butter or margarine in a heavy skillet. Add the chicken and stir constantly over moderate heat for about 3 minutes, or until the chicken is firm and white. Add the garlic and onions and cook for 2 more minutes. Stir in the flour and cook for 1 minute, stirring constantly.

Add the parsley, cream, Swiss cheese and Parmesan cheese and stir until blended. Remove pan from heat when cheese has melted and cream is hot. (Don't let mixture boil.). The total cooking time is about 6 minutes. Season with salt and pepper and serve over hot pasta or rice. Yield: 4 servings.

Pineapple Chicken

4 boneless, skinless chicken breast halves
1 tablespoon cornstarch
2 teaspoons cold water
1 teaspoon salt
1 teaspoon soy sauce or tamari

4 tablespoons vegetable oil
1 cup celery, chopped
1/4 lb. fresh snow peas or 1 package, frozen and defrosted
2 scallions, chopped into 1/4-inch pieces
4 slices canned pineapple (reserve juice)
1/3 teaspoon Season-All (optional)
1 tablespoon honey
Hot cooked rice

Cut chicken into approximately 3-inch long, 1-inch wide strips and marinate in mixture of cornstarch, cold water, salt, and soy sauce or tamari for 1/2 hour in refrigerator. Rinse snow peas if fresh and clip ends. Set aside. Slice pineapple into wedges.

Heat vegetable oil in a wok over high heat. Remove chicken from marinade. Stir fry chicken for 3 minutes in two separate batches. Then add all chicken back to the wok. Add celery, snow peas, and scallions, and stir fry together until chicken is lightly browned and vegetables tender. Meanwhile, mix together pineapple wedges, pineapple juice, Season-All and honey. Pour over browned chicken and vegetables. Simmer until hot and until chicken is no longer pink in the center. Serve with rice. Yield: 2 to 4 servings.

Chicken Roma

1/2 lb. hot Italian link sausage, 1/2-inch slices
1/2 lb. sweet Italian link sausage, 1/2-inch slices
1/4 cup flour
1/4 teaspoon garlic powder
1/4 teaspoon dried oregano
1/4 teaspoon salt
4 boneless, skinless chicken breast halves
2 tablespoons olive oil
1 medium onion, diced
1 green bell pepper, diced
1 red bell pepper, diced or 1 jar (2 oz.) diced pimientos
1/4 lb. mushrooms, sliced
3 cloves garlic, minced
1 (14.5 oz.) can Italian plum tomatoes, drained and halved (reserve liquid)
1/2 cup red wine
1 teaspoon chopped fresh basil or 1/4 teaspoon dried
Black pepper to taste

Brown the sausages in a large, heavy skillet over medium-high heat. Remove the sausages from the skillet with a slotted spoon and drain on paper towels. Combine the flour, garlic powder, oregano and salt. Coat the chicken in the seasoned flour. Sauté the chicken in the grease left in the skillet until browned on both sides. Remove the chicken from the skillet and set aside. Drain the grease from the pan and discard.

Add the olive oil to the pan. Stir in the onion, green pepper, red pepper, mushrooms, and garlic and sauté until golden, about 5 minutes. Return the sausages and chicken to the pan. Add the tomatoes, wine, basil, and pepper to taste. Cover and simmer over low heat for 30 minutes. Add the reserved tomato liquid if the sauce is too thick. Yield: 4 servings.

Chicken Scaloppini

12 boneless, skinless chicken breast halves
3 tablespoons olive oil
1 tablespoon oregano
1 tablespoon basil
1 tablespoon garlic powder
Salt and pepper to taste
3 cups onions, sliced
1/2 cup green pepper, sliced lengthwise
2 (48 oz.) cans of whole peeled tomatoes
2 lbs. of angel hair pasta (cooked)

Sauté chicken in olive oil. As chicken turns opaque, add oregano, basil, garlic powder, salt and pepper. When chicken is done and no longer pink in the center, add sliced onions and peppers, cover and cook for 10 minutes on medium heat. Add tomatoes and simmer for 45 minutes. Serve over angel hair pasta. Yield: 12 servings.

Chicken Sukiyaki

1 1/2 lbs. bone-in chicken breast halves
2 stalks celery
1 medium onion, sliced
1 teaspoon salt
4 tablespoons butter or margarine
1 bunch green onions, trimmed to about 3 inches long and sliced lengthwise
1 cup fresh mushrooms, sliced
1/3 lb. fresh spinach, cut in 2-inch lengths
1/2 cup celery, thinly sliced
1/2 cup bamboo shoots, thinly sliced
1/4 cup soy sauce
1/4 cup chicken stock
2 tablespoons sugar
Rice

Simmer chicken in water to cover, adding celery, sliced onion, and salt to the water. Cook just until tender enough to bone and slice. Cut from bone in slices. In a large skillet, lightly brown chicken slices in butter or margarine for about 8 minutes, 4 minutes on each side. Push chicken to one side or remove from pan. Add onions and mushrooms, and cook until lightly browned. Add spinach, celery, bamboo shoots, soy sauce, chicken stock and sugar. Cook until vegetables are just tender, but still crisp and chicken is no longer pink in the center. Serve with hot cooked rice. Spoon liquid from pan over each serving. Yield: 4 servings.

Provencal Chicken

4 bone-in chicken breast halves, skin removed
1/4 cup flour
1/2 teaspoon salt
3/4 teaspoon dried thyme
2 tablespoons olive oil
1 medium onion
1 garlic clove, chopped
1 cup chicken broth
8 large green olives, drained and pitted

Mix the flour with salt and 1/2 teaspoon of dried thyme a large resealable plastic bag. Add chicken pieces and shake to coat; set aside. Heat 1 tablespoon oil in a large non-stick skillet. Add the chicken pieces a few at a time and cook until evenly browned, about 20 minutes. Drain on paper towels.

Cut the onion into thin wedges. Add the onions and remaining 1 tablespoon oil to the skillet and cook, stirring until golden, 6 or 7 minutes. Add garlic and 1/4 teaspoon thyme; cook and stir for 1 minute. Add chicken broth and bring to a boil. Return the chicken to the skillet; add the olives. Cook for 15 minutes, covered, or until the chicken is cooked through and no longer pink in the center. Yield: 4 servings.

Pollo Con Calabacita

1 (3 1/2 to 4-lb.) chicken pieces
1/4 cup vegetable oil
2 large zucchini, cubed
1 clove garlic, minced
3 tablespoons flour
2 tablespoons onion, chopped
2 tablespoons green pepper, chopped
1 teaspoon salt
1 teaspoon pepper
1/2 teaspoon ground cumin
3 cups water

Heat oil in a Dutch oven until hot. Add chicken cook until browned, about 4 minutes on each side. Remove from oil and drain on paper towels. Discard pan drippings.

In a bowl, combine zucchini, garlic, flour, onion, green pepper, salt, pepper and cumin; toss gently. Return chicken to the Dutch oven and spoon vegetable mixture evenly over chicken; add 3 cups water. Bring to a boil; reduce heat, and simmer, uncovered, 40 to 45 minutes or until chicken is tender, stirring frequently. Yield: 4 servings.

Pasta-Chicken Combo

2 cups cooked chicken, chopped
4 oz. penne, uncooked
1 teaspoon sesame oil
1 1/2 tablespoons olive oil
1 1/2 tablespoons sesame oil
2 medium carrots, sliced diagonally
1 small purple onion, chopped
2 medium zucchini, halved lengthwise and sliced
2 cloves garlic, pressed
1 1/2 teaspoons fresh ginger, grated
1/2 teaspoon dried crushed red pepper
2 tablespoons soy sauce
2 teaspoons rice wine vinegar
Parmesan cheese, grated

Cook pasta according to package directions; drain and toss with 1 teaspoon sesame oil. Set aside. Coating sides, pour olive oil and 1 1/2 tablespoons sesame oil in a preheated wok or large skillet; heat oil on medium-high for 2 minutes.

Add carrots and onions; stir-fry 3 minutes. Add zucchini, garlic, ginger and red pepper; stir fry 1 minute. Stir in pasta, chicken, soy sauce, and vinegar; stir fry 1 minute or until thoroughly heated. Transfer to a serving dish; sprinkle with Parmesan cheese. Yield: 4 servings.

Chicken Cutlets with Sun-Dried Tomatoes

8 boneless, skinless chicken breast halves
2 tablespoons butter or margarine
1 white onion, thinly sliced
3 tablespoons sun-dried tomatoes, thinly sliced
1/4 cup cooking or dry white wine
1/3 cup water
8 slices mozzarella cheese

With meat mallet or rolling pin, pound each chicken breast to 1/4-inch thickness. Set aside. In a large skillet over medium-high heat, melt butter or margarine and cook chicken breasts until lightly browned on both sides, about 3 to 5 minutes per side. Remove chicken to platter and keep warm.

In the drippings in skillet, over medium heat, cook the onion until tender, stirring occasionally. Add sun-dried tomatoes, wine and water; heat to boiling over high heat. Return the chicken to skillet; top each chicken breast with mozzarella cheese; cover and cook over medium-low heat until cheese melts, about 2 minutes. To serve, spoon sauce over chicken. Yield: 4 servings.

Chicken Fettucine

4 boneless, skinless chicken breast halves, cut into 1-inch pieces
10 oz. uncooked fettuccine
3 tablespoons olive oil or margarine
10 oz. mushrooms, sliced
1 teaspoon garlic salt
1/8 teaspoon pepper
1 3/4 cups whipping cream
1/3 cup fresh parsley, chopped
1/4 cup grated fresh Parmesan cheese

Cook fettuccine per package instructions; drain. Meanwhile, in a Dutch oven or large skillet, heat oil or margarine over medium-high heat until hot. Add chicken and mushrooms; cook 6 to 7 minutes, stirring occasionally, until chicken turns white and is no longer pink in the center. Add garlic salt and pepper. Cook 1 minute.

Add cream and reduce heat to low. Cook 3 to 5 minutes, stirring constantly, until sauce is thick. Stir in Parmesan cheese and parsley. Add cooked fettuccine; toss to coat. Cook 1 minute, stirring constantly, until fettuccine is hot. Yield: 4 servings.

Orange-Glazed Chicken

1 lb. boneless chicken breast tenders
2 tablespoons margarine
1/4 teaspoon salt
1/8 teaspoon pepper
1/4 cup water
1 cup baby-cut carrots, cut in half lengthwise
2 cups frozen sugar snap peas
1/2 cup orange marmalade
1 tablespoon cornstarch

Meanwhile, in a Dutch oven or large skillet, heat margarine over medium-high heat until hot. Add chicken tenders; sprinkle with salt and pepper. Cook 3 to 4 minutes on each side, until golden brown on each side. Remove chicken from skillet; keep warm. In the same skillet, add water, carrots and snap peas. Cook, covered, on medium-high heat for 4 to 6 minutes or until crisp-tender.

In a small bowl, combine cornstarch and marmalade. Place marmalade mixture in skillet and add chicken; cook 2 to 3 minutes, stirring occasionally, until chicken is cooked thoroughly and no longer pink in center and sauce has thickened. Yield: 4 servings.

Easy Chicken Cacciatore

1 (4 to 5-lb.) whole chicken, cut into pieces, skin on
1 large onion, chopped
1 clove garlic, mashed
2 tablespoons olive oil
1 cup hot water
1 (6 oz.) can tomato paste
1/4 teaspoon salt
1/8 teaspoon pepper
1/2 cup mushrooms, sliced
1/2 cup tart red wine
Egg noodles or spaghetti

In a large skillet, cook onion and garlic in oil. Add chicken and brown on both sides for about 4 minutes on each side. Combine water, tomato paste, salt and pepper; pour over chicken. Add mushrooms. Cover and cook on low heat about 45 minutes or until chicken is cooked through and tender. Add wine and cook 5 minutes more. Serve over egg noodles or spaghetti. Yield: 4 servings.

Chicken Hungarian Goulash

1 lb. boneless, skinless chicken breast halves, cut into 1-inch pieces
2 tablespoons olive oil
1 (14.5 oz.) can chicken broth
1 (5 oz.) package (1 1/2 cups) uncooked elbow macaroni
1 (14.5 oz.) can stewed tomatoes, undrained, cut up
1 (8 oz.) can tomato sauce
1 1/2 cups frozen green beans
3 teaspoons paprika
1 teaspoon sugar

Spray a large non-stick skillet with non-stick cooking spray. Add olive oil and heat over medium-high heat. Add chicken; cook 3 minutes, stirring occasionally. Add broth and bring to a boil. Reduce heat to medium; add macaroni. Cover; cook 10 minutes.

Stir in tomatoes, tomato sauce, green beans, paprika and sugar. Cover; cook 5 to 10 minutes or until chicken is cooked and is no longer pink in center and pasta is tender. Yield: 4 servings.

Chicken Carbonara

2 cups cooked rotisserie chicken, skin and bone removed, chopped
8 oz. uncooked spaghetti
1 cup frozen baby sweet peas
3 slices bacon
1 (16 oz.) jar Alfredo sauce
1/4 cup grated Parmesan cheese

Cook spaghetti per instructions on package. The last 2 minutes of cooking, add peas. Drain; and return to saucepan.

Cook bacon until crisp; crumble. Combine chicken, Alfredo sauce and bacon with cooked peas and spaghetti. Cook over low heat about 5 minutes, stirring occasionally, until thoroughly heated. Sprinkle with Parmesan cheese. Yield: 4 servings.

Creamy Chicken and Apples

4 boneless, skinless chicken breast halves
1 medium onion, sliced
1 tablespoon vegetable oil
1/2 cup chicken broth
1/4 cup apple juice or water
1/4 teaspoon dried thyme
1/4 teaspoon salt
4 medium tart apples, cored and cut into 1/8-inch slices
1 tablespoon flour
3/4 cup half-and-half cream or evaporated milk
Hot cooked egg noodles

Flatten chicken to 1/2-inch thickness with meat mallet or rolling pin. In a large skillet, sauté onion and chicken in oil until chicken is lightly browned and onion is tender, about 4 minutes on each side. Add chicken broth, apple juice, thyme and salt. Reduce heat; cover and simmer for 10 minutes. Remove chicken and keep warm.

Add apples to skillet; cover and simmer for 4 to 5 minutes or until apples are tender, stirring occasionally. In a bowl, mix flour and cream together until smooth; add to skillet and mix well. Bring to a boil; cook and stir for 3 minutes. Pour sauce over chicken; serve over noodles. Yield: 4 servings.

Chicken and Angel Hair Pasta

3 boneless, skinless chicken breast halves (12 oz.)
1 (12 oz.) package angel hair pasta
1 tablespoon olive oil
2 cups broccoli florets
2 cups baby carrots
1/4 cup water
1 teaspoon chicken bouillon granules
1 (28 oz.) jar chunky-style pasta sauce
1/3 cup grated Parmesan cheese

Cook angel hair pasta per package instructions; drain. Cut chicken into 1-inch cubes. Cut carrots in half lengthwise. Heat oil in large nonstick skillet over medium heat. Add chicken; cook and stir 5 minutes. Stir in broccoli, carrots, water and chicken bouillon. Reduce heat to low; cover and cook 5 minutes or until vegetables are tender yet crisp and chicken is no longer pink in the center.

In a medium saucepan, bring pasta sauce to a boil over high heat. Place pasta on plates; top with hot pasta sauce and chicken and vegetable mixture. Sprinkle with cheese. Yield: 6 servings.

Pan Barbecue Chicken

1 (3 to 3 1/2-lb.) bone-in chicken pieces
3/4 cup onion, chopped
1/4 cup vegetable oil
3/4 cup ketchup
3/4 cup water
1/3 cup vinegar
3 tablespoons sugar
3 tablespoons Worcestershire
2 tablespoons mustard
1 teaspoon salt
1/2 teaspoon pepper

Brown chopped onions in oil in an electric frying pan. Add remaining ingredients for the barbecue sauce; heat. Add pieces of chicken and bake at 325 degrees F for half hour. Turn once and continue baking another half hour. Yield: 6 servings.

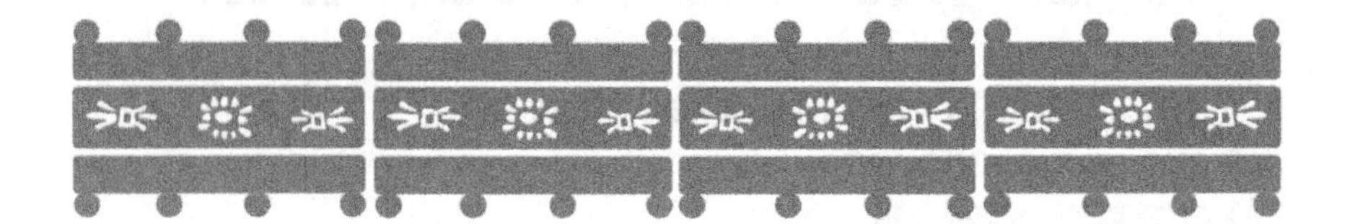

Microwave Chicken

Microwave Chicken

Moo Goo Gai Pan

8 boneless, skinless chicken breast halves
2 tablespoons oil
3 oz. snow peas
1/2 cups mushrooms, thinly sliced
2 tablespoons green onions, thinly sliced
1/2 cup water chestnuts
1 cup water
2 teaspoons instant chicken granules
2 tablespoons soy sauce
2 teaspoons cornstarch
1/2 teaspoon ground ginger
1/8 teaspoon pepper
Rice

Cut chicken into bite-size pieces. Mix chicken and oil in a microwave-safe casserole dish. Microwave, covered, on HIGH 8 to 10 minutes. Let stand covered 5 minutes. Add peas, mushrooms, onions and water chestnuts. Microwave on HIGH 4 to 5 minutes. Remove from microwave.

In a glass bowl, mix water, chicken granules, soy sauce, cornstarch, ginger and pepper. Cook on HIGH 3 minutes or until thickened; stirring every minute. Pour over chicken and stir well. Serve with rice. Yield: 6 to 8 servings.

Baked Chicken with Artichokes

1 (3 to 3 1/2-lb.) chicken pieces
1 onion, finely chopped
1/4 lb. mushrooms, thinly sliced
2 garlic cloves, finely chopped
1/3 cup flour
1 1/2 teaspoons paprika
1 1/2 teaspoons salt
1/2 teaspoon dried rosemary
1/4 teaspoon pepper
1/2 cup chicken broth
1/4 cup dry sherry
1 (6 oz.) can artichoke hearts, drained

Mix onion, mushrooms and garlic in microwave-safe dish. In a small bowl, mix flour, paprika, salt, rosemary and pepper. Coat chicken with flour mixture. Place chicken on top of mushroom mixture. Pour chicken broth and sherry over chicken and vegetables. Cook on HIGH for 10 minutes.

Move chicken pieces on outside of dish to center and center pieces to outside. Cook at 70% power for 12 to 15 minutes or until chicken is done. Gently mix in the artichoke hearts. Bake at 70% power for 3 to 5 minutes. Let stand 5 minutes. Yield: 6 servings.

Chicken Ratatouille

4 boneless, skinless chicken breast halves (thinly sliced)
1/4 cup oil
2 small zucchini, thinly sliced
1 small eggplant (peeled and cut in 1-inch cubes)
1 large onion, thinly sliced
1 medium green pepper (seeded and cut in 1-inch cubes)
1/2 lb. mushrooms, sliced
1 teaspoon dried parsley
1 teaspoon salt
1 teaspoon basil
1/2 teaspoon pepper
2 garlic cloves, minced
1 lb. tomatoes (peeled and cut in wedges)
Hot cooked rice

Heat oil in 2-quart microwave-safe casserole dish on 80% power for 2 minutes. Add chicken and sauté on HIGH for 4 to 6 minutes. Add zucchini, eggplant, onion, green pepper, mushrooms, parsley, salt, basil, pepper and garlic cloves; cover tightly.

Microwave on HIGH 5 to 8 minutes or until chicken is done and vegetables are tender crisp. Add tomatoes and stir gently. Microwave on 50% power 2 to 3 minutes. Serve with rice. Yield: 4 servings.

Honey and Sesame Chicken

1 (2 1/2 to 3-lb.) whole chicken, cut into pieces
1/2 cup butter
1/2 cup honey
1/4 cup lemon juice
1/4 cup prepared mustard
1/4 cup toasted sesame seeds

Melt butter on 70% power for 1 to 1 1/2 minutes. Add honey, lemon juice and mustard; stir well. Place chicken in 13x9-inch microwave-safe dish. Meaty portions of chicken should be placed to outside of dish. Pour honey mixture over chicken. Refrigerate for several hours.

Microwave on HIGH for 12 minutes. Rearrange chicken so less cooked portions are to outside of dish. Baste chicken with drippings. Microwave on 70% power for 10 to 12 minutes or until chicken is fork tender. Let stand for 5 minutes covered. Sprinkle toasted sesame seeds on chicken and serve. Yield: 4 to 6 servings.

Chicken Breast with Vegetables

4 boneless, skinless chicken breast halves
2 carrots
2 stalks of celery
2 small potatoes
1 medium onion (thinly sliced)
2 tablespoons butter or margarine
1/2 teaspoon salt
1/8 teaspoon pepper
2 tablespoons minced fresh parsley
Paprika

Cut carrots, celery and potatoes in julienne strips. Place carrots, celery, potatoes and onion in shallow 1 1/2 qt. microwave-safe dish. Dot with butter and sprinkle with salt, pepper and parsley. Cover with plastic wrap and cook on HIGH for 10 minutes, stirring halfway through cooking time.

Place chicken on vegetables on the outside of dish. Lightly sprinkle chicken with paprika. Cover with plastic wrap and cook on HIGH for 10 minutes or until chicken is done and no longer pink in the center. Yield: 4 servings.

Stuffed Chicken Breasts

4 boneless, skinless chicken breast halves
1 cup seasoned stuffing, crushed
1/2 cup grated Parmesan cheese
1 tablespoon dried parsley
1/2 cup butter, melted
2 slices thin sliced ham
2 slices American processed cheese

Mix together stuffing, Parmesan cheese and parsley. Dip chicken in butter, then roll in stuffing crumbs. Take half slice each of the ham and cheese; wrap around breast and place skin side up in 9-inch microwave-safe baking dish. Repeat with the other three breasts. Sprinkle remaining crumbs and butter on top of chicken. Cover with wax paper, and cook for 10 minutes on HIGH in microwave. Turn dish once. Yield: 4 servings.

Chicken and Dumplings

2 1/2 lbs. chicken pieces
2 cups water
6 whole peppercorns
2 bay leaves
2 teaspoons salt
3 medium carrots, peeled and sliced thin
6 tablespoons flour
3/4 cup cold water
1 teaspoon sage
1 (4 oz.) can mushrooms, drained
1 (10 oz.) package frozen peas, thawed

Dumplings:
1 cup Bisquick
1/3 cup milk
2 tablespoons parsley flakes

Place chicken, water, peppercorns, bay leaves and salt in a deep 2 1/2 qt. microwave-safe baking dish. Cover and place in microwave on HIGH for 13 minutes. Stir and cook for 7 additional minutes. Add carrots and cook, covered, for 7 minutes. Remove chicken and cool; cut into bite-size pieces. Return to baking dish. In a small bowl, combine flour, 3/4 cup water and sage. Gradually stir into chicken mixture. Heat, covered, for 7 minutes.

Prepare dumplings:
Mix Bisquick, milk and parsley flakes. Add mushrooms and peas to chicken mixture. Drop dumpling dough by spoonful on top of chicken mixture to form 6 dumplings. Heat covered 5 minutes. Uncover and heat 4 to 5 minutes longer until dumplings are no longer doughy on bottom. Yield: 4 servings.

Chicken Parmigiana

2 boneless, skinless chicken breast halves
1 egg
1/4 cup water
1 cup seasoned dry bread crumbs
1/2 cup grated Parmesan cheese
4 slices mozzarella cheese or 1 cup (4 oz.) shredded
2 tablespoons oil
1 cup spaghetti sauce

Beat egg with water. Mix Parmesan cheese and bread crumbs together. Dip chicken in bread crumbs mixture, then in egg and again in crumb mixture. Coat bottom of 8-inch microwave-safe dish with 1 tablespoon oil; add chicken to dish and sprinkle chicken with remaining 1 tablespoon of oil. Cook on HIGH 3 to 4 minutes; turn chicken, cook on HIGH an additional 3 to 4 minutes.

Top with spaghetti sauce; cook on HIGH 6 to 8 minutes. Cover each piece of chicken with sliced or shredded cheese. Let stand, covered, 5 minutes until cheese melts or return to microwave for 1 minute on MEDIUM to melt cheese. Yield: 2 servings.

Other Books by Bonnie Scott

100 Easy Recipes in Jars

100 MORE Easy Recipes in Jars

Pies and Mini Pies

Holiday Recipes

Simply Fleece

Soups, Sandwiches and Wraps

Slow Cooker Comfort Foods

Fish & Game Cookbook

Cookie Indulgence: 150 Easy Cookie Recipes

100 Easy Camping Recipes

Camping Recipes: Foil Packet Cooking

All titles available in Paperback and Kindle versions at Amazon.com

Photo credits

Photos by

Vadimmmus, photos.com

Jacek Chabraszewski

Leslie Elieff

Graphics by

Cheryl Seslar

Made in the USA
Monee, IL
06 August 2024